Promoting Reflective Teaching

Promoting Reflective Teaching

Supervision in Practice

GUNNAR HANDAL AND PER LAUVÅS

The Society for Research into Higher Education
& Open University Press

76063

Published by SRHE and
Open University Educational Enterprises Limited
12 Cofferidge Close
Stony Stratford
Milton Keynes MK11 IBY, England

and

242 Cherry Street Philadelphia, PA 19106, USA

First Published 1987

British Library Cataloguing in Publication Data

Handal, Gunnar
  Promoting reflective teaching: supervision
  in practice
  1. Teaching
  I. Title II. Lauvås, Per
  371.1'02   LB1025.2

  ISBN 0-335-15547-2

  ISBN 0-335-15546-4 Pbk

Library of Congress Cataloging in Publication Data
Handal, Gunnar.
    Promoting reflective teaching: supervision in practice
    Bibliography: p.
    1. Teaching.   2. Teachers——Training of.
I. Lauvås, Per, 1942-   II. Title.
LB1025.2.H2945   1987   371.1'02   87-22108

ISBN 0-335-15547-2
ISBN 0-335-15546-4 (pbk.)

Project management: Clarke Williams
Printed in Great Britain

Contents

List of Illustrations   vii

Preface   ix

1 Introduction   1

2 The 'Practical Theory' of Teachers   9

    The content of the 'practical theory'   9

    The influence of a practical theory on teaching practice   15

    The degree of consciousness about one's practical theory   16

    Focus in counselling: development of practical theory   17

    Who is right?   19

    What is practice?   25

    Summing up   28

3 Counselling in Practice   30

    The counselling document   32

    The content of the counselling document   34

    Three phases in counselling   36

    Process-intentions for counselling   43

    Summing up   48

4 Basic Principles Underlying the Counselling Strategy   50

    The precedence of the teacher's practical theory   51

    Counselling for independence   51

    The exemplary character which underlies counselling   52

    Counselling as 'discourse'   55

    Counselling as neither confrontation nor prop   56

Counselling as critique   61
Roles involved in counselling   62
Meta-communication: a tool and a professional standpoint   67

5 Relationships, Themes and Perspectives in Counselling   73

Relationships   74
Themes   76
Perspectives   81

6 Implementation of the Counselling Strategy   87

Problems in counselling in general   87
Problems of implementing the proposed stategy   90
Problems related to various fields of application   95

7 Summary of the Main Points   105

References   109

Index   113

The Society for Research into Higher Education   115

List of Illustrations

Figure   **Page**

Figure 2.1   The Practice Triangle   26
Figure 2.2   Relationship between practice and practical theory   28
Figure 3.1   Pre- and post-session counselling   43
Figure 7.1   The counselling process   107

Preface

. . . that one, when it shall really be possible to lead a person to a specific place, first of all has to find where he is and start from there. This is the secret of the art of helping. Anyone who is not able to do so is simply seducing himself into believing that he is able to help others. To really help another person I must understand more than he does, but first of all understand what he himself understands. When I don't do so, my superior understanding does not help him at all. When I still want to impose my superior understanding, then it is because of my vanity or pride, in that I don't really want to help him but want him to admire me instead.

However, the true art of helping starts with a humiliation. The helper must first humiliate himself under the one he wants to help and thereby understand that to help is not to be the most imperious but the most patient one, that to help is the willingness to accept being wronged and not understanding what the other one understands. (Kierkegaard 1859, authors' transl.)

A chameleon is an animal which, according to experts in the field, is characterized by:

— The ability to adapt to its surroundings by changing its colour to match the colours around it.
— Extremely rapid, independent eye movements (it is capable of looking ahead with one eye while the other one is looking up, down or backwards).
— Cautious movements as if it is testing the surface.
— Vigorous defence of its own territory.
— A need of shelter at night when its changing of colour no longer serves as a defence mechanism.

In East Africa the Chameleon is believed to bring misfortune, as it is supposed to be a medium for evil spirits.

Chameleons don't teach; neither do they counsel — at least not so far as we know! Still we have found it appropriate to introduce this strange animal to the reader from the very beginning. The reasons for doing so will be given later on in the book; and we hope that the theme throughout it will be apparent and related to this metaphor. We think there is a lesson to be learnt from the animal: supervision may develop chameleon behaviour because that is the only intelligent thing to do as a response to inadequate supervision. On the other hand, successful supervision is what takes a trainee (teacher or student) *beyond the chameleon game*.

The main message of this book is that counselling (which takes place in supervision or in consultancy work for teachers or instructors) must be based on the teacher's own conditions and take as a starting point the teacher's own 'practical teaching theory'. In the quotation which we have chosen as the vignette for this book, Kierkegaard writes about his own writing. We find it highly valid for counselling as well.

We are referring to counselling as a process in which a supervisor is working together with people under training to become teachers, pre-school teachers, instructors, etc., or when a consultant is working together with people who are already employed in functions like these and who want to develop better ways of carrying out their functions. To us, counselling is a process in which the counsellor's task is to contribute to the development of the people s/he is working with, so that they can carry out their educational responsibilities and tasks in a professional and independent way.

We have tried our best to develop a *strategy* for counselling. Our own background for doing so is partly theoretical — based on our work in the Division of Social Pedagogy at the Institute for Educational Research, Oslo. In addition, we have extensive practical experience from counselling teachers and instructors working in various types of adult and tertiary education. We also have extensive experience in conducting courses and seminars for trainers; that is, the staff of counselling centres, organizations for adult education, industrial companies, teacher-training colleges and universities. We have had the opportunity to consult other people working in the same field, such as European colleagues in staff development in higher education.

The theme of the book is not supervision in one, confined and specific situation. Our intention has been to present a general strategy which can be adapted and applied in a variety of educational settings. Reference is made to supervision during teacher training, when students at teacher-training colleges practise teaching. Reference is also made to consultancy work carried out by a consultant, advisor, head or colleague in order to promote professional development in some kind of in-service training. Reference is made to co-operative efforts among teacher colleagues who try to improve teaching standards in their school or their community. Some aspects of the supervision of teachers in their further education are also covered. Other areas of application are listed in Chapter 6.

It should also be observed that supervision is a vital element in all kinds of job-related training. However difficult it may be to design and implement theoretical training programmes for various jobs, it is still our conviction that the greatest challenge in this area is to achieve an appropriate programme for helping trainees put into practice their theoretical knowledge and their acquired skills in the actual job situation. In too many training programmes, theoretical and practical training tend to live independent lives, and it is more or less left to the student to bridge the gap between the two. Supervision is supposed to assist the student in doing so, but there is obviously a long way to go yet before appropriate standards have been reached. Although our focus is on teacher training, we do hope that this book offers some guidelines and principles of interest to those involved in designing and implementing training programmes in other areas as well.

At this stage the terms *counselling, training* and *consultancy work* will be given initial definitions. *Counselling** is an activity within the wider framework of the process of qualifying for a profession or a specific job, through training or vocational practice. It is limited to those situations when one — or some — of the participants is — or are — teaching and others are taking part in analysing, discussing, assessing, giving advice, and criticizing plans for teaching or implementation of teaching. This activity is by no means sufficient as the *education* necessary to qualify for teaching or instruction. In this book, however, our scope is restricted to counselling, and does not include all other aspects of teacher education. In addition, teacher education will have to include *studying* (time to read, discuss, listen and think) as well as *training* (time to practise skills needed in teaching). *Consultancy work* is an in-service activity for teachers who are seeking professional assistance to develop or change their own working methods. In this case, the clients are both competent and experienced and are free to engage, as well as to dismiss, the consultant.

One aspect of teacher education not covered in this book is the *evaluation* of teaching practice. We have addressed the question of how to make supervision fill the role it is supposed to have in training and further development, and not how it can be utilized as a tool to control or assess teaching standards. A brief discussion on assessment is, however, included in Chapter 6.

At this point we should like to make a grateful acknowledgement. We are professionally and personally indebted to Ole B. Thomsen, who was formerly in charge of the Institut for anvendt universitetspedagogik (Institute for applied studies on university education) at the University of Copenhagen. He has now left this field and is working within a different area. In 1975 he published a mimeographed paper, 'Evaluation and counselling of teachers on teaching practice', in which he launched some ideas that made us start thinking differently. He focussed upon the criteria for such evaluation and counselling, and showed through his analysis how closely these criteria are connected to different theories and philosophies of teaching, although they do not appear to have such connections in the way they are usually presented and applied. On this basis, he

---

*Our preference is to use the term 'counselling' instead of 'supervision'. To us, 'supervision' implies a distinct superior/subordinate relationship which may reflect the situation in some parts of pre-service training programmes adequately, but not at all when it comes to in-service training and consultancy work.

'Counselling', on the other hand, carries a connotation of a psychological perspective, which is not our prime concern. However, we have chosen the latter term in this book to denote the process of facilitating the professional development of teachers, whether they are teacher-trainingstudents, teachers at various levels of the educational system or instructors outside the formal educational system.

suggested the candidate's own *intentions* for teaching as the prime criterion against which evaluation ought to be made and from which counselling should start. It is fair to say that this strongly influenced our own theory and practice in counselling. We have tried subsequently to develop and augment these ideas in an effort to build up for ourselves a theoretically sound strategy for counselling which at the same time would work in practice.

We have asked Ole B. Thomsen to read a preliminary version of this book and we are happy to report that he recognizes his own ideas. Whatever has happened to them through our intervention should not be blamed on him. The original ideas were his alone and we gratefully acknowledge their great influence on our own work.

Gunnar Handal
Per Lauvås

1

Introduction

A tutor who tooted a flute
Tried to teach two young tooters to toot.
Said the two to the tutor,
'Is it harder to toot, or
To tutor two tooters to toot?'
(Carolyn Wells, quoted by Cerf 1960)

Counselling is an ancient way of introducing a novice into a trade and passing on the skills from one generation to the next. For a long time it was the only way to train craftsmen. It is till a teaching method of high reputation, although modern training programmes contain a wider variety of learning processes and teaching methods.

Judging from current practices, little training and few guidelines are apparently required to counsel students under training in most cases (it is only quite recently that special training has been required for people taking on such a function in Norway and this is, as far as we know, an exception). Normally, a skilled person is considered competent to supervise as long as he knows the job.

While teaching in so many cases takes the form of transmitting information, with the teacher occupying the leading role, counselling is a form of training in which the learner is placed in focus. The counsellor cannot limit his task to the transmission of *his* own understanding but must take the skills, knowledge and values of the learner as the point of departure.

Counselling is also characterized by close and direct contact between supervisor and learner. In this respect, it provides a favourable environment for learning. At the same time it implies that those taking part get fairly close to each other in matters of personal significance. From our experience, and for various reasons, counselling requires a specific strategy and particular skills compared to other teaching methods.

It is a puzzling fact to us that so few books have been published on counselling as a teaching method. Compared to the number of volumes dedicated to other teaching methods, curriculum design and development, evaluation and so on, the statistics indicate a discrepancy between the frequency of counselling and the interest shown in it by the professionals in the field.

Counselling takes place in many training programmes and educational contexts: in skills training, practicals, writing exercises, on-the-job training, tutoring for scientific work, the training of specialists and so on. Besides, there is formal — and even more informal — counselling among colleagues and by superiors in many practical fields. It is with both these settings in mind — counselling during training and at work — that we have developed our counselling strategy.

In this book we want to focus on counselling as part of teacher training. We have selected this field so as to focus on just one *example*. 'Teachers' include everyone who takes on the role of teacher or instructor within the formal educational system or outside this system and, even if the examples given are mostly taken from training situations, we do think that the same lines of reasoning are valid for counselling as part of consultancy work with practising teachers.

Our experience so far supports the idea that a number of counselling situations have so many common features that the basic ideas presented can be applied in training programmes other than teacher training. We have confidence that the ideas are relevant to the training of medical doctors, nurses, physiotherapists, managers, engineers, etc., just to mention a few. With the task of developing a *counselling strategy relevant to different settings* in mind, it is — we hope — possible to accept this book as being about counselling *in general*. We have not primarily aimed at a description of how the process of counselling should be adjusted and tailored to fit the quite different organizational 'frames' or contexts within which it takes place. We also recognize the structuring effects of institutional frames on educational processes. Organizational and situational elements have certainly to be taken into consideration and given much attention when a counselling strategy is translated into a specific procedure. However, in spite of all the possible contextual differences, counselling with teachers can be described as a unitary process with its own dynamics and characteristics.

In this book we have therefore tried to identify the constitutive characteristics of this counselling process. Our point is that a proper identification of them should precede an analysis of the relevant elements in any specific organizational framework. Deviations will always occur from the counselling process conceived as an ideal. Necessarily, the strategy when applied at all has to be adjusted to the situation in question. However, we must make the point that organizational structures which bear on counselling should be exposed to the same critical attention as the counselling strategy itself and be justified to the same extent.

There is not always a perfect correspondence between the labels applied to teaching methods and what actually takes place in the teaching process. A 'seminar' does not identify a specific activity. At our university the label 'seminar' changes meaning when crossing from the Humanities to the Natural Science faculty. In many cases, labels applied to teaching methods are understood differently by different individuals and, even more so, by different groups and cultures. How does this observation apply to 'counselling'?

From our observations in a variety of training programmes where counselling is carried out, counselling is often very close to a 'one-to-one lecture' or demonstration. One who knows how to do it explains to one (or a few) who does not know and who is therefore learning how to do it. When supervisors explain what counselling in fact *is*, the description often does not correspond totally to the observations.

However, let us point to some characteristics of counselling, distinguishing it from other teaching methods.

Student activity

Student activity is essential — not only mental activity, listening and taking notes. The student should in fact be carrying out the activity and the work processes, practising the do which he is supposed to learn. The task of the supervisor is not to do the job *for* the student but to help the student to master the job he is practising.

Let's take an example. Imagine the supervisor in a plant receiving a trainee for on-the-job training. In cases like this, the supervisor will *do* and *explain* the job with the trainee *looking* and *listening*, perhaps asking some questions. The fact is that the trainee has been taught about pumps, say, earlier in his training programme, so there is really no strong need to go over all this once more. But the supervisor was not there when the trainee learned about pumps and does not know what the trainee knows already. He goes on explaining while dismantling the pump:

> You see, before we can do anything, we have to close the valves on each side of the pump and drain it so that it is disconnected from the flow line. And, as you probably know, this is a displacement pump and the thing that is normally wrong with a pump like this is . . .

And so on. The supervisor in this case should keep in mind the Turkish proverb: God must have had something in mind when he created man with two ears and only one mouth.

The supervisor should let the trainee do the job. In order to prevent the trainee from causing any damage and from making a fool of himself, he should first ask him to explain what he will do, how he will carry out the job and why he wants to do it that way. It is the thinking of the trainee that matters and the trainee's own practice that is important, not the supervisor's own talking and demonstrating.

The supervisor's role, consequently, should be that of helping the student to get the work done correctly. He should correct any improper work operations and ideas, encourage the student to do his best in order to experience achievement, elaborate upon the aspects not fully appreciated, help him to break down a complicated task into its constituent skills and have him practise each component and put them together. The idea is that the trainee will *understand* better as well as being able to practise the particular skills after this period of training.

Openness of professional criteria

In some cases, supervision is concerned with the shaping of behaviour towards an ideal pattern. Examples can be identified in sports coaching where a consensus has been reached on the ideal patterns and sequence of movements. Some specific work operations are of this kind.

In most cases, however, the assumption that there is only *one* correct performance is not valid. A good coach or supervisor will know that there have to be variations in the idealized patterns for different individuals. And, what is more, in many cases there is no ideal pattern at all, but there are general criteria for job performance and some more or less vaguely defined professional standards indicating the line between acceptable and unacceptable job performance. Within the area of acceptable job performance, it is up to the members of the work force to work out for themselves their individual work style, reflecting personal values, personality and experience.

It is not a straightforward task to coach/supervise ski jumpers, dancers, golfers, tennis players and the like, as this is in professional work which is *not* governed by the same kind of limited behaviour-span and the same kind of agreed-upon norms of performance. Being a supervisor, one will inevitably apply the norms developed through one's personal, professional development, well aware of the fact that colleagues of the same profession hold somewhat different values, have somewhat different priorities, do things somewhat differently and so on. So, how is it possible to foster independence and responsibility within the rather wide boundaries of acceptable role behaviour, and not merely achieve the acceptance and copying of the behaviour of a supervisor?

Teaching — the main focus of this book — is a profession characterized by this openness of performance criteria. Counselling must therefore be carried out in such a way as to encourage the students to make a personal stand on the basic aspects of the profession and to assist in their attempts to profile a teacher role which fits their potential.

Practice

Supervision is linked to practice periods within a training programme. In some programmes the practice periods are placed towards the end of the programme, while in others they are placed in the middle and in some cases they are distributed throughout the later part. There does not seem to be one perfect way of distributing theoretical and practical periods.

When the practice periods are placed at a late stage, a marked gap between theory and practice tends to develop over time. The teaching staff become specialized in either theory or practice, communication between the two groups tends to deteriorate; differences in status start growing and it becomes a task for outsiders and the beginners themselves to take responsibility for the practical training.

Practice periods are, however, highly important parts of most training programmes. This is the official stand of most educational institutions; however, in the day-to-day priorities, nothing like the same attention is paid to practical training as to the theoretical aspects of the course.

The relationship between theory and practice is often considered to be a problem of proper sequencing, which it is not. Early practice is good because it might make the student aware of the requirements of later work and thereby given perspective on later studies and the need for theory. But early practice is also bad because it might be considered a paradox to the trainee to practise skills which he has not yet been taught. Late practice is good because it allows a gradual introduction to the work with access to the help of experienced people. But at the same time it may be bad because socialization into the profession has gone too far and has mainly taken place in a theoretical sphere.

In sum, the relationship of theory and practice is dialectic and not a matter of sequence. Each practice period must be placed in the training programme for a specific purpose in order to bridge the gap between the two spheres.

Supervision is mainly related to the practical part, but the general purpose is to make theory relevant to practical work and to prepare students to act as professionals. In order to achieve this, the *quality* of practice periods has to be considered.

The question of how to make supervision in practice periods effective is of concern in this book.

Freedom from action

In a real working situation, it is necessary to make decisions about what to do all the time — often with practically no time available to figure out what is the most sensible thing to do. Even when in severe doubt one cannot freeze the situation in order to think. While theorists can sit in their offices, far away from the pressing needs of action, spending days and weeks analyzing what goes on in the practical world, identifying principles and structures to create order in a blurred world, the practitioner often finds himself in a constant, immediate decision-making and acting role.

Freedom from action is the privilege of the academic disciplines of education. While the practitioner gains in experience from acting and from reflecting upon the action and its consequences, the task for the academic community is to search for simplicity in complex activities and situations and to develop theories which can be of help to the practitioner who does not have the same opportunity to step back from the situation.

In a way, this distinction may be applied as a characteristic of counselling. The student is introduced into the world of action but does not remain there. During counselling sessions she* retires from the sphere of action to the contemplative world where opportunities and assistance are offered to analyse the social, educational processes in which she is taking an active part. The practitioner (student, teacher, etc.) gains experience in any case through alternating between action and reflection. The main purpose of counselling is to enrich the reflection phases of the practitioner. The underlying idea is that an experienced person can be of substantial assistance in this respect.

Our concern has been to make *explicit* a strategy in such a way as to *make it accessible to both sides* in the counselling process. It is our firm belief that counselling is performed more succesfully when the intentions, practices and rules of the game are agreed upon by the participants. What is more, when a counselling strategy is made explicit, it is possible — although not always likely — that the person being counselled will make her own needs known to the counsellor as regards the desired outcomes of the counselling.

Our focus throughout the book will be mainly at what we can best term the micro-level. However, what goes on in counselling sessions is, to a great extent, influenced by outside forces and can only be properly understood in an organizational and societal perspective. It has been our ambition to keep the text close to the perspective of the practitioner in the field, with fairly detailed accounts

---

*The feminine pronoun is used intentionally, as we explain later (p. 7).

of practical procedures and examples to illustrate the points made. We are aware of shortcomings in these respects, but we suspect that the greater shortcoming relates to the societal perspective on the issues, which has perhaps not been made sufficiently prominent.

Our main topic is that of a *strategy* for counselling. However, the counselling process also has a content aspect to it: it is *about* something. There is, naturally, a connection between the two aspects of strategy and content. The strategy which is applied determines to some extent what is considered to be relevant contents to be dealt with, and vice versa. This holds for the strategy we are proposing. However, as the reader will have the opportunity to observe, there is no tight correspondence between the underlying assumptions about education reflected in our strategy, and the ones reflected in our sketches of content. As a counselling strategy, our approach might perhaps best be labelled 'humanistic' or 'dialectical', while our dealings with content might be labelled partly 'technological' and partly 'critical'.

When reading our sketches of potential counselling content, you may wonder whether there are pupils or students in the schools or other institutions we are referring to. We admit that we have written far more extensively on the relationship between the counsellor and the teacher than about teachers and students. After all, this is a book on counselling with teachers. However, our reasons for not writing much about pupils and more about objectives, content, frames and so on, have to be explained.

The task of a teacher is very much a social one. But it is more than merely a social activity. The teacher has to transform a social situation into an educational process. In order to do so, she has to adopt a professional frame of reference. After some time in the profession, this frame of reference may be adopted more or less automatically by the teacher. However, when counselling is involved, its major function is to make the professional frame of reference (in which concerns about students should hold a central position) quite explicit and the application of it a matter of the first importance.

What we would like the reader to have in mind, when judging the appropriateness of the proposed strategy, are the 'degrees of freedom' that exist within the strategy. It is not necessary at all — not even desirable — that users of the strategy apply as content the same analytical categories, the same themes and the same perspectives that we are suggesting. What we refer to in these matters reflects the preferences — and possibly even biases — we have had during our own practical work in the field. So, we are not suggesting that the content outlined in later sections (especially Chapter 3 and 5) represents *the* questions that should be dealt in the counselling process.

However, we do insist on the strategy itself. To us, it is really the strategy that matters. Therefore, we deal more extensively with the theoretical foundations of the strategy than with those of the content, where no coherent theoretical framework for our choices will be offered.

There exist several books on educational counselling (see, for example, Lewis and Miel 1972, Goldhammer *et al.*, 1980, Stone 1984) as well as on counselling in similar professions, for example social work (Killen Heap 1979). What, then, is the point of writing a new book on this topic? It is because there are radically different ways of thinking about counselling. Our book does not differ to any considerable extent from other books as far as the technical aspects are concerned. Goldhammer *et al.* have similar steps or phases in the counselling process (although they include and additional step, intended to give feedback to the counsellor). Lewis and Miel place far more emphasis on counselling from an institutional perspective and have some excellent chapters on counselling at a micro-level (for example on criticism).

Our basic view — and we sincerely hope that this is reflected throughout the text — is that the counsellor should *assist* in developing teaching competence. It is the teacher's own conscious development and growth that matters. This position — however hard to explain in a few lines — has strong implications for both strategy and its consequent procedures.

It is a private and odd experience of the authors that it has been far easier to talk about the contents of this book that to write it. This is not meant as an excuse for what we have written. We only want to emphasize to the reader the need for him to do his own thinking and to invite colleagues to discuss these matters. We would have enjoyed very much participating in such discussions!

As we shall note in more detail later (particularly in section 4.7), counselling involves different roles, primarily those of the counsellor and the 'counsellee'. For the first role we have adopted the usual name. For the second — the one who is 'subjected' to counselling — we have, however, decided to use the term *teacher*. Although some of those who take this role are not formally teachers (they may for instance be students in training), we deal with them in counselling in their role as teachers, and have accordingly adopted this collective term for them.

The personal pronouns used in a context like this are also a matter of importance. As language can be a powerful factor in the relationship between the sexes, there is some risk of exerting undesirable pressure by verbal means. We have decided, therefore, to refer to the teacher as *she* and to the counsellor as *he*, except in some examples where male teachers are involved. As we identify more strongly with the counsellor's role — through our practice — and as we are both men, this usage is natural for us. It also has the advantage of providing different pronouns for the two participants in counselling, and thus happily avoids confusion in the text.

Reading the book, you will probably find that the same themes recur different places throughout the text. This repetition is deliberate, as we consider it important to talk about central issues in different connections, to show how they have application and value when presented from different perspectives. You may also find that the illustrations or examples given are picked up from a number of different fields where counselling takes place: teacher training, adult education, university teaching etc. Some of these are, of course, outside your immediate area of concern. Our reason for doing this has been to try to show how counselling — even when applied in a variety of fields — has a central core of elements which are basically the same, and on which we want to focus. So do not let the diversity of the examples distract you from the central points they are meant to illustrate. Our intention is exactly the opposite.

Chapter 2 presents the main thesis of the book, as well as some theoretical considerations underlying the strategy.

Chapter 3 contains a description of the steps and procedures of counselling in practice. Apart from being intended to serve as a guide to counselling in day-to-day situations, the description in Chapter 3 is also meant to serve as a concrete frame of reference for the following chapters.

Chapter 4 contains the most prominent principles for the work of a counsellor. From our point of view, Chapters 2 and 4 contain the essence of the book. It may be of some interest to notice the 'Chinese-box problem' involved in our writing about the issues which are included. One example will suffice.

In section 4.8. we make some comments on the need to alternate between communication and meta-communication; as an important aspect of counselling, we employ it in the book as well. You will therefore find sections of meta-communication throughout the text. Our hope is that these will have some of the value in *this* connection that they are supposed to have in counselling sessions, because of the 'exemplary' character of both processes, that is, their character as exemplars (see section 4.3).

Chapter 5 suggests elements of a potential content to be included in counselling sessions. Again, let us stress our choice of the word *potential*. The perspectives and themes presented merely reflect signposts in *our* present practical theory. Disagreement with out practical theory of *teaching* need not automatically lead to a rejection of the *counselling* strategy.

Chapter 6 contains some notes on implementation problems. These, however, are not extensively covered. For appropriate implementation within a specific institution, there are certainly more considerations to be taken into account than we have mentioned. We would like to draw attention to two points. Firstly, in teacher training, counselling is normally connected with evaluation for assessment purposes. *We*, in contrast, have concentrated upon counselling as an instrument for the further development of the teacher's professional practice and not as a tool to control or assess the results of that development. It is not difficult to imagine assessment procedures that can make it very difficult to adhere to the basic principles of really productive counselling. (A brief discussion of this issue is given in Chapter 6.3.1.)

Secondly, it may be very difficult to create a counselling situation that secures the necessary degree of emotional and social support outlined in section 4.5. Creating an atmosphere of sufficient support takes time and requires a reasonably stable, interpersonal relationship. When arrangements that help to secure a satisfactory interpersonal climate cannot be made, there are likely to be detrimental consequences in the shape of more confrontation than the teacher can take.

Finally, Chapter 7 contains a summary of the main points.

2

The 'Practical Theory' of Teachers

In this chapter we will introduce the main *thesis* of this book — and of a strategy for counselling with teachers. Then we will establish some of the *pre-conditions* which we think are important for understanding and eventually accepting the thesis.

> *Thesis*: Every teacher possesses a 'practical theory' of teaching which is subjectively *the* strongest determining factor in her educational practice.
> Counselling with teachers must consequently originate in each teacher's practical theory, seeking to foster its conscious articulation, and aiming to elaborate it and make it susceptible to change.

To give meaning to this thesis, however, it is necessary to look in more detail at the meaning of the term 'practical theory' as it is used here.

The content of the 'practical theory'

The term 'theory' commonly refers to an interrelated set of hypotheses or statements which can be used to *explain* or understand phenomena or situations, or to *predict* what will happen when certain conditions or premises exist. This is the scientific use of the term. What might be the proper use of the term in education is a disputed question which we, however, will not discuss here.

In this book, 'practical theory' refers to a person's private, integrated but ever-changing system of knowledge, experience and values which is relevant to teaching practice at any particular time. This means, first of all, that 'theory' in this sense is a personal construct which is continuously established in the individual through a series of diverse events (such as practical experience, reading, listening, looking at other people's practice) which are mixed together or integrated with the changing perspective provided by the individual's values and ideals. In this way, a 'practical theory' may be regarded as a complex 'bundle' of all these elements. It is also worth stressing that it is indeed a *practical* theory, primarily functioning as a basis or background against which action must be seen, and not as a theoretical and logical 'construct' aimed at the scientific purposes of explanation, understanding or prediction.

Although such 'theories' held by different people may have a high degree of similarity, there will always be a personal or individual aspect to them. Personal experiences in practical teaching situations (as teacher or as pupil) will differ from person to person, even though the same general kind of experience is common to many individuals. The books read or the lectures listened to may be identical for many students at a teachers' college. Nevertheless, the knowledge gained, and the meaning and the consequences extracted from these sources, will vary among— them. Consequently, we do not have in mind just one or even a few 'theories' that people who teach hold and which guide their practice. We use the term 'practical theory' to refer to the indefinite number of 'bundles' of knowledge, experiences and values which have been and are continuously established in people, related to teaching (or to educational practice generally).

It is probably necessary to go a little further into this concept and — for analytical purposes — to dissect it, trying to identify more clearly its elements as well as their interconnections. For analysis, let us establish three components included in this 'practical theory':

— personal experience
— transmitted/mediated knowledge, experience and structures
— values (philosophical, political and ethical).

Personal experience

All young people and adults have experienced educational situations, at least as pupils being educated, taught or trained; many also have had further experience as educators, teachers or trainers. Consequently, we have all experienced practice which was, variously, successful, dull, terrifying, rewarding, difficult, and so on, and have — to a variable extent — drawn personal conclusions as to why things were experienced as they were. These experiences, conclusions and hypotheses accumulate and form part of our practical theory. In formal teacher training, specific situations are set up to provide experience in the kind of teaching for which the training officially prepares. At a minimum, such teaching practice will give the 'raw experience' of having taken part and performed a role in teaching situations. At its optimum, it will also give rise to an understanding of the situation and of the student teacher's own role in it, of why things went as they actually did; and even an understanding of more general phenomena in education, seen in the light of this particular experience.

Experience of this kind may — according to Bateson (1972) — lead to learning at different levels. At the first level, we learn what to do in similar situations; in ohter words, we learn the content of the 'lesson'. At the second level, we learn a lot about the relationships and structures which are implied but not explicitly stated. We learn about ourselves as persons, about the roles we are expected to play, and so on. Often, this kind of learning is both more subtle and more fundamental, and, accordingly, well worth taking into consideration when looking into a person's practical theory.

The quality of the experience we get out of a teaching/learning practice varies considerably. It may add much or add little to our personal practical theory. If what happens in the actual teaching practice is elaborated afterwards, preferably in the light of one's own and other people's experience and knowledge, there is good reason to believe that the *understanding* added to the practical theory will be richer than if the practice is only experienced and not explicitly reflected upon. It may be helpful to notice that the concept of 'praxis', as used by the 'Frankfurt School', consists of two constitutive elements of *action* and *reflection* upon action. To put it another way: some fishermen are said to have twenty years' experience of fishing; others have only one year, experienced twenty times. The latter have never reflected enough on their practice to actually learn from it. Could the same also be said about teachers?

Transmitted knowledge, experiences and structures

In addition to what we directly experience ourselves, and thus can use as material for our theory building, we pick up and include other people's experiences and knowledge as well. The visiting teacher who comes to our staff meeting to describe his way of teaching a particular subject or topic, the course-book put together by experienced authors, the research report from an educational development programme, the ideas about ways of dealing with pupils who have learning difficulties communicated by a colleague over a cup of tea in the senior common room — all these are sources upon which we draw to expand and 'fortify' our 'theory'. In none of these cases is our own immediate personal experience in a practical situation involved, although relating to such experience may make these contributions more meaningful and valuable.

Included in this component are also those structures which are transmitted to us in the form of concepts, theories, commonly-held beliefs, and so on, whether they are transmitted by persons, by the media or by way of the material world surrounding us. When the word 'teacher' in common language is meant to indicate a person who transmits knowledge to someone else, we have an example of language structures which influence our practical theory, as in the structuring effect of a specific theory of motivation or a prejudice about race relations. Through their influence on our practical theory, they affect our actual practice.

Values

Our own values, or ideas of what is good and bad in education as well as in life generally, are probably strong determining elements in our practical theory. We may have a preference for a competitive or a co-operative relationship between people. We also have specific attitudes to authority. We have different ideas concerning the value of classical subjects as opposed to training for mastery of daily-life situations as the appropriate 'content' for education. All this will no doubt have a strong influence on the way our personal practical theory is constituted — and, accordingly, on our teaching practice. The values in question may be of a more general ethical or philosophical nature concerning the 'good life' (for instance, that a meaningful life is preferred to an abundant life), they may be political values (like ideas about democracy, the distribution of values, freedom and the power of influence) or they may be more directly related to education (like equality of educational opportunity, the right to receive teaching in accordance with one's culture, and so on).

Integration of the elements in a practical theory

The brief comments and examples which appear under the last three headings may lead us to believe that this complex entity labelled 'practical theory' is in fact a simple phenomenon, neatly subdivided into three categories available for inspection. This is far from The truth. The division above is meant only for analytical purposes. The different 'parts' of the theory are — in reality — intimately interwoven and impossible to identify as isolated categories in a person's practical theory. They are influenced by — as well as influencing — each other in the continuous modelling and remodelling of the theory.

Not all the elements have necessarily the same weight or importance in the integration process. This is probably best illustrated by looking at the influence of values on the two other categories. Values, as we know from psychology, heavily influence our perceptions of things we experience ourselves, as well as what we perceive and accept in ideas presented by others. We sort out, delete and integrate, interpret and distort received impressions on the basis of what we hold to be good and right. A similar structuring effect on our new experiences (personal as well as mediated) is created by our earlier experiences.

This leads us to perceive and use the knowledge transmitted to us from others in the light of what we value, as well as in accordance with the perspective created by earlier experiences. Thus the values we hold will — directly and indirectly — have a dominating effect on the structuring of our practical theories.

On the other hand, we experience our own practical efforts very much in the light of structures, concepts and theories transmitted to us, in such a way that this may even lead us to change our values and beliefs to some extent.

Another relevant distinction worthy of note is the one made by Ryle (1945) between 'knowing how' and 'knowing that'. The distinction implies a difference between theoretical knowledge about a phenomenon or a procedure (for instance teaching) and practical knowledge as to how to perform or to act (for instance, again, in teaching). It is indeed possible to know a lot *about* an activity without being able to practise it oneself.

A person's practical theory — it will be seen — may be balanced so far as these forms of knowledge are concerned, or it may be heavily 'overloaded' toward one of them.

If, for instance, the practical theory consists excessively of 'knowledge that', this may be due to the fact that it is based more on mediated knowledge transmitted from others, and less upon personal experience in relevant practical situations. For counselling, this means that a certain part of the basis for the theory — in this case the experiential part — ought to be favoured. If the opposite emphasis of the theory is the case, counselling should provide possibilities for the teacher to put her practical 'know-how' on a footing of more generally acknowledged concepts to make the total, integrated content of her practical theory more valuable. Ryle's pair of concepts thereby helps us to realize again the importance of the necessary dialectical relationship between action and reflection in any individual's production of authentic knowledge.

Some other concepts may be helpful in understanding this complex integration of elements into a practical theory. We have adopted them from Arfwedson (1985) who is, in turn, indebted to Bernstein (1971), Lundgren (1972) and Sarason (1971). They say that the teacher is dependent upon a *code* (principles for ordering their conception of the school) which, in each particular situation, will determine the way they perceive the school-world around them (*perception of surroundings*). This perception, again, gives rise to their particular way of *acting*, which in turn may lead to experiences contributing to either a confirmation of (or a change in) the *code*. The code is therefore a product of both former and new experiences as teacher or pupil — and accordingly a product of socialization. What goes on around the teacher in the educational world (*in the context*) is experienced in the light of her present *code* in such a way as to fit into her *perception of the surroundings*. In order for her to develop further, and to change her code, counselling may be needed as a productive element in the school situation, questioning the code and confronting it with conflicting evidence as to its adequacy.

Another term comparable to our 'practical theory' is '*strategy*' in the way it is used by Stenhouse (1979). He too stresses the integrated character of any valid basis for action established in the teacher's thinking, comprising knowledge from philosophy, learning theory, developmental as well as social psychology, and sociology — as well as practical experience. Stenhouse, however, does not include our kind of value element in his concept of a teaching strategy, leaving out, to our mind, an important element in the integrative structuring of the strategy — or of the practical theory, as we prefer to call it. In sum, we must regard this practical theory as a dynamic and ever-changing 'bundle' of these elements based on both practice and what, in other uses of the word, might be referred to as 'theory', integrated within a value-perspective.

Practical theory as an individual or collective entity

Up to now we have referred to the practical theory as the individual teacher's construct, upon which their practice is based. In our context this will also be the predominant perspective. However, we think it is possible to apply the term even when we are dealing with *groups* of teachers and the basis for educational practice that they share. In counselling with, for instance, the staff of teachers at a particular school (or with a faculty of teachers in a university department), this is an important use of the term to bear in mind.

Just as a particular teacher may be said to have developed at a given time a practical theory for teaching, a group of teachers, working together in an educational institution, may have had experience shared between them, as well as shared knowledge from readings, lectures, courses, and so on. They may, in addition, have some values which are central to them all and around which their collective practical theory is integrated. In reality, however, such collective practical theories will in many cases be quite rudimentary, owing to the fact that only a small part of the educational practice in schools is shared. It is, in fact, possible in many types of schools for teachers to go on practising side by side, on the basis of quite different practical theories, without too many conflicts between them. It is an accepted part of educational tradition that teachers are allowed a great deal of 'professional freedom' in their work. From the pupils' point of view, however, such discrepancies in practical theories among their teachers may be quite an exhausting element in their school experience. They are the ones who constantly have to adjust to differences in practice due to differences in the theories which prescribe that practice.

In schools where teachers have sought and found co-operation (or have been 'forced' to co-operate because of an open-plan school environment) the situation may be different. Co-operation provides mutual insight into one another's practice, and may give rise to questions and discussions about the reasons underlying such practice. For any kind of co-operative teaching to develop, some collective practical theory must be established among the partners in the enterprise. This may happen as a result of complementary domination and submissiveness without any explicit discussion and decision-taking between the teachers involved. It may, however, also be the result of a long and continuous dialogue on the educational questions involved, resulting in the development of a collective practical theory that is shared among the co-operating. It goes without saying that this is not an easy, conflict-free process. Rather, it is likely to be demanding and controversial, as differences in experiences, knowledge and values have to be resolved (at least to some degree) for the group to arrive at some viable collective basis for their work. Counselling which tries to help the members of the teaching team become aware of the differences between them, as well as aware of the contradictions implicit in the situations in which they work, may be helpful in the development of such a collective basis for action.

Here we are dealing with a similar phenomenon which Arfwedson (1979) has referred to as a *collective code* as opposed to an *individual code* for each teacher.

It will not be possible in all cases for, let us say, the total staff of teachers in a school to agree on a collective practical theory which embraces all of them and, at the same time, includes enough common knowledge and values to be productive in practice. A minimum requirement in such situations, however, ought to be that the different prevailing teaching practices, as well as their related practical theories, are *known* to the different members of staff, so that they can be taken into consideration in the overall planning and implementation of the work of the school.

It may be useful at this point to refer to authors like Lortie (1975) and Sarason (1971) with regard to the present status of such collective practical theories. When teachers as a group have not succeeded to any extent in establishing a collective theory for their work, this is very much due to the fact that such success presupposes some collective insight into practice as well as collective reflection upon it. This pre-condition, however, involves more time devoted to working together at school than has traditionally been required of teachers. Becoming engaged in a practice of this kind would mean reducing the freedom of the individual teacher to plan and reflect, and would accordingly mean placing a personal constraint on the normal work of that teacher.

In most of what we shall be writing about further on, we return to the counselling of individuals to improve their individual practical theory. We regard it as important, therefore, to refer to collective practical theories as relevant entities in counselling with groups as well, and will return to the topic briefly in Chapter 6.

The influence of a practical theory on teaching practice

At this point there may be good reason for asking ourselves the question 'What are actually the important "governing factors" for educational practice?' Are we governed to a large extent by our ideas of good teaching, our theory, ideals, thinking and planning — in short, by our practical theories — or are other factors more influential? What about the social pressure stemming from our colleagues or from the pupils and their parents? Or what about the influence of the 'frame factors' such as the curriculum, the architecture of schools, the rules and regulations enforced upon us from above, the resoures we have at our disposal, and so on?

When asking teachers about the factors which influence the character of their teaching practice most strongly, we often receive answers indicating that frame factors and social factors — particularly at a local level — are perceived by the teachers as more influential than their own 'practical theory'. This has also been empirically demonstrated in Sweden (Arfwedson 1985). From a Marxist point of view, it might be valid to consider the practical theory as an ideological entity established to make the structurally and materially governed practice meaningful and acceptable to the actors concerned and to society.

Whatever our theoretical framework, it is possible to support the statement that work in schools is strongly influenced by factors outside the command of the individual teacher or group of teachers; We concur with this view and accept the research and theory illustrating and demonstrating it.

So why focus so strongly on working with teachers' practical theories — with their minds — as we are doing in this book, when mind probably matters less than matter? We think there are good reasons to do so.

Firstly, although the frame factors of different kinds have a strong impact on educational practice, these factors are also 'moulded' through the way they are interpreted and understood by the teachers who are doing the teaching. Although the architecture of the school and the size, form and equipment of its rooms will definitely limit forms of teaching, we still see that different groups of teachers are able to utilize such potentials rather differently. They seem to 'see' and understand their surroundings differently, thus psychologically operating in different environments although these may be quite similar materially.

Arfwedson (1985) has shown that the 'code' of teachers — their principles for interpreting the world around them as well as for acting in it — is influenced by the context in which the teachers work. Although this is true, it may also be possible to influence the individual code or the school code through the introduction of systematic counselling — for instance in the way introduced in this book — as a 'context factor'. To summarize, the frame factors do not only govern teaching directly. but mainly indirectly throught the way they are interpreted and understood by the teachers working within them.

Secondly, the frames imposed on the school by forces outside it still leave quite a sizeable 'freeroom' open for the decisions of the teachers. Within this freeroom the teacher has the option of making choices and decisions, and — as demonstrated by Berg and Wallin (1983) — most teachers do not utilize this freedom to its full extent. Rather, many of them stay within frames and limits imposed on them by their own lack of imagination, knowledge of alternatives, and so on. This freeroom, consequently, is an important part of the arena for counselling, where change is possible through the changes of teachers' individual and collective practical theories without entering into conflict with limiting material and structural frames.

Thirdly, counselling can assist in the process of making frames of different kinds visible and apparent to teachers. Making such factors conscious is at least a step in a process whereby they may eventually be changed, if that is considered necessary. Changes of this kind, however, will rather be a result of political or organizational work than of the individual work of teachers in their daily teaching.

Consequently, we do not deny the effect of frame factors in influencing strongly what happens in teaching. On the contrary, for reasons given above we *also* find it important to work with the minds of those who interpret the frames in daily ife, who act with some freedom within the imposed framework and who may even be actors in the everlasting battle to decide which frames to impose on the school.

When focusing on working with teachers' practical theories, it is important to bear in mind that we are working within the set of mental 'brackets' outlined above. We do not claim that teaching can only — or even mainly — be changed by changing teachers' minds through their practical theories, and this is our main focus, in this text.

The degree of consciousness about one's practical theory

It is necessary to emphasize that, by saying 'all teachers have a practical theory,' we here literally mean all those who set out on the task of teaching others, whether they have any professional training for it or not. That means that we include students at a teacher-training institution the moment they first meet a class of pupils, as well as fully-trained and experienced teachers who have been practising for years. We also include those who teach only as a minor part of their vocational function, e.g. people from different professions who take on a teaching role as part of, or in addition to, their ordinary jobs. Hence, the 'theory' we speak of here is not something reserved for trained and certificated teachers in the profession, being the result of their official preparation.

From a casual inspection only, it is noticeable that this practical theory is not only different as far as content is concerned. It differs also in its degree of *elaboration*, as well as in the extent to which it is *consciously* held by the teacher concerned.

In instances when the role of a teacher is performed we can see that there is a very limited consciousness of the practical theory underlying teaching practice. Some will even deny having such a theory, and will therefore be unable to formulate important parts of it. Still, some sort of theory exists in their thinking and will influence the way they teach, even though this influence may be less than conscious. Their values, their own experiences in similar situations of what 'works', as well as what counts for them as knowledge about teaching, will form a basis which influences what they actually do in their own educational practice.

Even teachers who recognize that they have a practical theory which determines their work will often have problems trying to formulate it. The composite nature of the 'theory', which we have tried to describe above, and the fact that it is not an explicit set of rules or prescriptions but is rather a 'bundle' of knowledge and evaluations makes formulation of it difficult in any simple, straightforward terms.

For many teachers — or teachers-to-be — the degree of elaboration of their practical theory (or its internal consistency) is not very high. Knowledge based on quite different sources, and with mutually inconsistent assumptions underlying it, may exist side by side and influence different parts of one's practice. This may be difficult to accept, as we have already pointed to the complex dynamic and integrating tendency which we encounter in the establishment of a practical theory. We believe, however, that this lack of consistency may be due to the fact that the knowledge, experience and values involved are often only partly understood and therefore poorly integrated; the basis of or assumptions underlying such knowledge is not readily apparent to the teacher. This knowledge is probably taken too much at face value and will, consequently, not be properly integrated. This will lead to inconsistency in the 'theory' which, again, will produce inconsistent or incompatible practice.

An important aim in counselling with teachers is, in our opinion, in making the practical theory of the individual teacher more conscious and elaborated. This implies

— helping the teacher realize what kind of knowledge and values underlie her practice,
— clarifying the reasons and justifications of significance to her,
— confronting her knowledge/values with alternatives outside, or already imbedded in her practical theory, and
— facilitating the teacher's own identification of internal contradictions and conflicts within her own practical theory.

For a teacher to become capable of expanding and refining personal practical theory, it is a great help to make that theory visible and accessible in its existing form.

Focus in counselling: development of practical theory

In our perspective, counselling deals with the development of the theory behind action, and does not focus primarily upon 'visible' teacher behaviour. An example may explain why.

Mrs Higgins, the geography teacher, receives in her class five students coming on teaching practice from the nearby college: John, Nanette, Fiona, Mark and Leslie. She wants them to learn how to teach map-reading and tells them to practise a technique of leading the whole class in reading the map by means of the teacher's presentation on an overhead projector. When actually implemented, this advice soon demonstrates that John is able to perform this kind of teaching with ease. He also understands and accepts Mrs Higgins's reasons for using this method, namely that the pupils have to get it right the first time when they start their map-reading in order to avoid misunderstandings and later re-learning. Nanette is also able to practise the kind of teaching required because it has been spelt out in some detail, but she has no understanding of why this might be a good way of doing it. She could, consequently, do it again in another teaching situation, but it might well be a situation where the technique would be absolutely irrelevant. Fiona, however, understands well, and accepts the reason for choosing the method and where and when it might be applied, but she is not yet able to perform in this role with ease. She is still a bit confused in her handling of the technical equipment, goes a little too fast in her explanation, but will certainly be able to master the technique, given a few more chances to practise.

Mark, on the other hand, masters the technique immediately and finishes his lesson smoothly, but he does not agree with Mrs Higgins's reasons for choosing that way of teaching. He keeps this to himself, and carries out the teaching as instructed. Finally, Leslie objects openly to Mrs Higgins on the same grounds as Mark, and decides to attack the teaching task quite differently: she leaves it to pairs of pupils to try finding out things from the map as a source of information. She also gives reasons for this alternative method, referring to her own way of looking at knowledge and her ideas about motivation in learning.

Several points can be made on the basis of this description of a practical situation.

Similar kinds of teacher behaviour may be the result of rather different practical theories, as in the case of John and Mark, who both perform well but on the basis of different practical theories.

Quite different ways of teaching may also be the result of similar practical theories, as is shown by Mark and Leslie, who would agree to a large extent about what would be the right thing to do in this particular teaching situation. However, they *act* here quite differently, evidently because Mark's theory also contains a tendency (or value) to conform or act as instructed, if it is unavoidable. There is reason to believe that they would teach in very much the same way if they were left on their own.

Neither Fiona nor Leslie carried out the teaching successfully, judged by Mrs Higgins's standards; but, on looking back, we see that there are very different reasons for their 'failure' — to be found in the realm of practical theory and in their consciousness of it.

A lot of the counselling that goes on in the practical part of teacher training focuses on training student teachers to master methods or techniques without giving sufficient attention to the underlying practical theory upon which this practice is based. According to our ideas of counselling, this means concentrating on overt student behaviour rather than on building the practical theory of the teachers involved. This emphasis may lead to some apparent short-term effectiveness, but not to the development of really professional practice in the long term. We think that Dewey, many years ago, pointed to the same truth in this quotation (1904, p. 28):

. . . criticism should be directed to making the professinal student thoughtful about his work in the light of principles, rather than to induce in him a recognition that certain special methods are good, and certain other special methods are bad. At all events, no greater travesty of real intellectual criticism can be given than to set a student teaching a brief number of lessons, have him under inspection in practically all the time of every lesson, and then criticize him almost, if not quite at the very end of each lesson, upon the particular way in which that particular lesson has been taught, pointing out elements of failure and success. Such methods of criticism may be adapted to giving a training-teacher command of some of the knacks and tools of the trade, but are not calculated to develop a thoughtful and independent teacher.

One cautionary note, however, is necessary at this point. The focusing in counselling on development of the teacher's practical theory does not, of course, preclude working on the mastering of techniques and methods for use in teaching. Every teacher needs to master such 'knacks and tools of the trade', and this accordingly must be part of a professional training. The important thing is to ensure that this part of the training takes place within the proper perspective — that of developing the understanding of teaching through the development of the teacher's practical theory. What is mastered in the area of techniques must be connected to, and integrated within this vital theory.

Summing up, we may say that the same teaching practice may reflect rather different practical theories (in content and degree of consciousness) and that similar practical theories may result in quite different practice. The training in practical ways of teaching does not, therefore, necessarily lead to a concomitant change in the practical theory underlying teaching behaviour. The chance to practise teaching is a necessary but not at all sufficient element in teacher training. Consequently, focusing training on the mastery of specific techniques must not be confounded with counselling, as we use the term. In order to improve the chances of changing teaching practice through counselling it is certainly the 'theory' underlying that practice which must be focused upon.

Who is right?

What now of Mrs Higgins's practical theory? Because *she* has one as well, of course. We have seen that it did not correspond to Mark's and Leslie's. Which of them is the 'right' one? Some of you will already have agreed with Mrs Higgins, while others will be backing up Leslie. And this is only on the basis of the very limited information we have given in the example. Further clarification might change the picture, but still we would be likely to have different opinions about who was 'right'. One alternative, in deciding, would be to give the 'right' to Mrs Higgins. After all, she is the counsellor in this situation, she has many years of experience and is the one who has both authority and authorization for the job. The problem, however, is that Mr Ross, who teaches geography in the neighbouring school, and who also receives students on teaching practice, would go along with Leslie in her view and support her solution and its justification. In this case, we must probably lean on real scientific educational theory to solve the conflict. What does research say? Again the problem is that research is not unambiguous.

We might find research showing that the mastery of a task is more quickly achieved when the correct performance is shown and the learner is trained to copy it. We may, on the other hand, find evidence that pupils who get a chance to explore their way into a new area are more highly motivated, learn more and with better retention than those who are led through the content step by step by the teacher. This may lead us to look in more detail at the evidence to see if the tasks or learning required are of a different nature in the two situations; whether what is meant by 'mastery' or 'knowledge' is different; or whether there are concomitant learning results (like, for instance, a development of dependence/independence) that also occur in either of the situations and that we would welcome or regret. There might be more to learn both for Leslie and John — and probably also for Mrs Higgins and Mr Ross — by looking into, as well as behind, the immediate reasons *why* we want to teach and why we actually teach the way we do. At least we would then be operating on the level of practice theory, where the *reasons* for our practical are to be found, even though they are sometimes hidden, unconscious and poorly organized.

The *immediate* problem in counselling (and even more so in evaluation) in teaching may seem to be to decide on who is to be the master — who has the right to say what is 'right' or 'wrong'. However, the way we see it is that the *real* problem in counselling is to learn how to allow the counsellor and the teacher to go together into the realm of 'what to do and why to do it' in order to explore the appropriate basis for action and the knowledge, experience and values supporting or contradicting different solutions. The aim of such an exploration is not to find out *who* is right, but to learn more about ways of thinking and acting in education in order to develop our own practical theories, to make them more consistent and to ensure that the use of them is a more conscious use. Lewis and Miel (1972, p. 234) put it this way:

> '. . . there is an increasing agreement in the profession that there is no single best way to teach; there are many ways. The important thing is to help the teacher to become self-propelling and self-actualizing.'

It should also be noted that what is meant by 'good teaching' is most certainly a controversial question. We may limit ourselves to evaluation in accordance with immediate criteria of effectiveness, in relation to limited objectives for a particular lesson; or we may see teaching against the background of what is good and therefore needed in a wider societal context. In taking the latter perspective, we may also differ in our criteria depending upon whether we are complying with the officially stated needs of society or whether we have a critical attitude towards those needs. Whether teaching is 'good' or not can thus be measured against very different standards: these ought to be discussed in counselling to make teachers aware of them, rather than making teachers conform to one standard by concealing the alternatives.

What we have just said might imply that we think that one kind of teaching is as good as another so long as the teacher is able to justify it in consistent terms. We don't. Both of us have our own preferences for 'the right way' in particular situations, and we sometimes even have difficulties in providing a solid justification for them. Two lines of argument have to be followed to explain this. The first we choose to call 'the-nature-of-education-argument' and the other is named 'the-what-do-I-do-when-no-one-is-watching-argument'. Let us follow them briefly before we return to the position of the counsellor in counselling practice.

The question of the *nature of education* is certainly a risky venture for anyone who is not a trained philosopher. So this is not going to be a thorough philosophical discussion of the question, but rather a brief sketch of some central points. Education is certainly no 'natural phenomenon'. It is on the contrary an artificial, cultural creation, which — even though it exists with similar functions in all cultures — takes on different shapes, aims and ideals from culture to culture and from time to time. The education in medieval schools for the aristocracy was quite different from that in today's state schools for the majority. The schools for teenagers in Newcastle-upon-Tyne, in Leningrad or in Guatemala may have striking similarities but still represent quite different ways of looking at education. Even within one country you will find quite different conceptions of the school and the way it ought to be run, which results in quite different teaching practices. What is 'good education' or 'good teaching', therefore, must be related to the group for whom it is supposed to be good (teachers and/or students, groups in society, and so on), as well as to some ideal of what is really 'good' for this group, and to the reasons why this is so.

Of course, it is possible to come to some sort of agreement on what we, in a particular society and at a particular time, should establish as our teaching system. On the one hand, this will only be an agreement at a high level of generality which will need a lot of further interpretation by teachers and school authorities. On the other hand, this is always an agreement reached under particular social and historical conditions which are subject to change and development. Even within settled periods between any formal changes in the framework of a school, changes in teaching ideals as well as in conceptions of what constitutes 'good teaching' may occur. Given this perspective, we find it difficult to base either teaching about teaching or counselling with teachers on a determinate model of 'good teaching', which is conventionally that assumed by those who work within teacher-training and which is used as the criterion against which teaching practice is evaluated. On the contrary, we consider it reasonable to focus upon an improvement in the teacher's conscious knowledge, about the relationship between what the teacher does in practice and the reasons for it, in order to become increasingly aware of her own theory and able to judge alternatives in a way which makes both rejection of them as well as revision of their own theory possible. In other words: for a teacher to be able to take a conscious stand in any future conflicts regarding her teaching practice, must have already internalized such conflicts and learnt to handle them, and not been merely taught specific 'correct' solutions to them.

Consider also the dependence of teaching on situational factors which are constantly changing. Good teaching does not come about in one way only. Given a certain group of pupils, a certain 'history' of what has just happened, a specific attitude existing in the group for the moment, and so on, the best way to teach a particular problem in mathematics may be quite different from the best way in some other situation. In addition, the personality of the teacher, the strong and weak points, what treatment the class is used to and the prevailing attitudes in the culture around the school are factors influencing what it might be 'right' to do. Still, among all this multitude of situational elements, a teacher must find a way to implement what has been established as her aims and objectives (at least in a long-term perspective) in accordance with the chosen philosophy. Even when this means that the teacher must *act* quite differently in different situations, she must be continually pursuing the same aims and keeping in line with her ideals. In other words she will try to teach according to a strategy, not just utilizing specific tactics or techniques more or less mechanically. To do this, she needs insight and under-standing and the habit of continually investigating what she really wants to achieve, how she is trying to bring it about and what experiences she is gaining. Teaching is an activity where there is no single way to the goal, but a very large number, and where many of these ways will suffice in any specific situation with its particular characteristics. This line of argument may well lead us to be classi-fied as value-relativists. Maybe this is a fair description. We mean that, in a field like education, it is important to have people working who are aware of the background of what they are doing, and who are able to change and adjust both their 'theory' and their practice in the light of new evidence, and reflect upon what really happens around them in the classroom, the school and society. Teachers who have learnt only to accept one model of teaching as the right one will more easily run the risk of either becoming rigid and static in their teaching or becoming passengers on any educational bandwagon that happens to pass by their school. Many different ways of teaching may be 'right', depending upon the time and the place in which it takes place, the elements to be found in the immediate situation, the aims which are being pursued and the ethical, political and educational values that the teacher is trying to implement.

Perhaps this represents an extreme view on our part, compared to other mem-bers of the educational profession who will probably take a less relativist stand in this matter. Some will say that educational theory has to be far more prescriptive than we allow. Others will claim that educational practice itself offers the advice which we argue is needed in our type of counselling process. Our stand — which no doubt reflects relativism and a disbelief in the direct application of educational theories or directives derived from day-to-day teaching practice — implies a belief in the vital importance of the teachers' professional judgement.

The other line of argument we suggested above was that dealing with the question 'what-do-I-do-when-no-one-is-watching'. We think this concerns the relationship between action itself and the basis for action. In teacher-training it is possible, and to some extent fairly easy, to get student teachers to model pre-scribed teaching behaviours. This is done in many teacher-training programmes and has been a tradition for some time. Examples may be found clearly in, for instance, micro-teaching programmes, where teachers are trained to perform specific techniques (like formulating questions to pupils or securing responses from a majority of the pupils in the classroom, and so on). This is done by means of bits of practical teaching in 'micro' situations (micro as far as the task, time and the number of pupils in the 'class' are concerned). The session is recorded on videotape and then played back to the teacher practising, preferably with a coun-selling teacher also watching and commenting. After the playback and coun-selling, the actual teaching sequence is repeated in order to get an improved result. The tasks and techniques selected for this sort of training are decided upon by those in charge of the programme and — at least sometimes — are based upon some theory or less systematic opinion as to what are considered important techniques to be mastered in teaching. This approach, of course, also rests upon values, knowledge and experience; and is subject to the same relativistic verdict as *any* theory.

Techniques learnt in this way may well be used in further teaching by those who have been trained to master them; but — in our experience — only to the extent that the teachers in question has accepted them as *hers*. This acceptance may, of course, be due to the fact that there are no alternatives that seem applicable in her teaching, or to mere belief in authority, rather than to thorough understanding of and agreement with the thinking behind the technique. If the techniques are not accepted, however, there is no reason whatsoever for the teacher to continue using them in further practice. The stronger the pressure is, in the training situation, to teach according to specific prescriptions (for instance through the use by tutors of a strict grading or evaluation system), the easier it will probably be to make the teacher conform to the rules while in training. However, the chances that teachers will continue to teach this way in their further vocational practice will be hardly likely to correspond to the certainty ensured by pressure during their training. Apart from the fact that they have had a chance to practise a certain way of teaching and will possibly resort to it where there is a lack of alternatives, teachers, like most other people, will be more likely to act according to their own beliefs or in their own interest, when not being watched, than to do what they have been told.

A reservation at this point is, nevertheless, essential. We do not consider educational situations as 'free' ones where the actors may do as they please. On the contrary, we regard teaching as an activity which is to a large extent framed by rules, regulations, structures (material and social) and resources. Still, there is a great freedom left to the teacher as a professional person to act as an individual, particularly when there is interest in exploiting the 'free space' within the system. And it is within this space where there is freedom for various practices that we maintain that teachers will prefer to act according to the conviction, knowledge and experience which is their *own*, a part of themselves, rather than to follow prescriptions given by others, the value of which they do not accept. The possible exception may be the extremely conforming teacher who is happiest looking for models in figures of authority. In our opinion, the school should certainly not base itself on this kind of teacher in the way it sets up its counselling system and procedures.

It is sometimes wise — although it may at the same time be a frightening thought — to consider the relative shortness of the period a teacher is in a formal training situation, compared to the length of time in real teaching. With an active vocational career of, say, forty years, the training period of three or four years is only a tenth of the vocational period — the tip, as it were, of the iceberg. Considering that counselling, in the form here described, is itself only a small part of the activities offered during training, one should probably not over-state what can actually be learnt as a result of teaching practice supported by counselling. The consequence for us of this consideration is to focus counselling on helping the teachers to develop independence and reflection *on her own*, together with an inclination to continue the development of her practical theory — again *on her own* — by the systematic integration of practical experience, transmitted knowledge and reflection upon both within an overal value perspective.

The same problem can be regarded from another point of view — that of educating for innovation. Stenhouse, in his inaugural lecture on Research as a Basis for Teaching (1979, p. 11) says:

> Teachers must be educated to develop their art, not to master it, for the claim of mastery merely signals abandoning of aspiration. Teaching is not to be regarded as a static accomplishment like riding a bicycle or keeping ledger, it is, like all arts of high ambition, a strategy in the face of an impossible task.

We agree with his notion that teaching must — throughout a career — be the development of a type of practice, not a falsely assumed mastery of it. Counselling must take this into account and aim at supporting the teacher's development. With reference to Abelard, Stenhouse (1979, p. 1) quotes the ideal of setting out 'to learn the wisdom which we do not possess'. If this is a task for practising teachers, counselling must be a help to them, not a hindrance, on their difficult way towards it.

Continuing from these two lines of argument, even if we do not think that *any* way of teaching is as good as any other, we still prefer to base our counselling with teachers on a thorough discussion or dialogue with the teacher about the basis for her practice and relationship between this basis and what the teacher does or plans to do. Even though we are pretty sure *ourselves* what we would prefer to do in a given practical teaching situation, we do not think it either *right* or *wise* to establish our solution (however well based in 'theory' we think it is) as the model to be followed. This is particularly so in counselling with *teachers*, considering the nature of the field in which they are working, although our thinking has relevance in other counselling situations as well.

We are, however, touching here upon a very delicate point in our argument — one which has certainly been pointed out by some of our students. It is that, as you yourself, in the role of counsellor, have your own practical theory, — aren't you more or less bound to impose it on the teacher? This imposition may, of course, be done so subtly that in practice neither party will be aware of it, and it may thus be just cleverly disguised manipulation. The risk is certainly there. To us, it is of vital importance to try to avoid it.

There is, it must be said, an inevitable tension involved in counselling. On the one hand, the counsellor may act completely on the basis of the teacher's own intentions and practical theory without expressing his own views or practical theory at all. On the other hand, he may force his own theory and ideals upon the teacher, either directly through manifest pressure or by subtle manipulation.

This is probably a major problem in counselling, whatever strategy is applied. As a counsellor, you will always be in a powerful position. You may find yourself enforcing your theory directly or you may find the same happening by manipulation. However, we believe both tendencies should and *can* be reduced.

The teacher must be able to go to the counsellor as a detached professional person. At the same time, she must be invited to relate herself to his theory, continuously and openly, as an alternative theory to learn from, relate to and even reject. This means that the counsellor and the teacher must know and realize the difference between *persuasion* and *conviction* (Hellenes 1975). The first is limited to talking someone into a new position either by virtue of one's authority or by arguments which may seem to be acceptable but which in fact are not really shared by the one who is being persuaded. This is a superficial change of position which will not result in a lasting change of practice, but only in an apparent change. Conviction, however, leads to the real acceptance of a position based on a recognition of the value of the arguments supporting it.

In practical counselling, accordingly, care must be taken to keep this distinction clear in minds of those involved. Just as it is right that the counsellor should argue, comment, present alternatives, make his own position clear, and so on, it should be equally clear that it is up to the teacher to integrate, disregard, connect, change or keep her own practical theory and make her own decisions about her practice.

One important reservation has to be made. The relationship between the teacher and the counsellor is not a totally symmetrical one with both participants in equal positions. And, at least in a training situation, an extra responsibility rests with the counsellor which, in certain situations, may lead him to object that some teacher-decision is being put into practice. He may, for instance, find the practice suggested unethical in relation to pupils. However, this is something that should be stated frankly and not disguised as an artificial 'consent' between the teacher and the counsellor. The asymmetric relationship in this situation must be declared in order to establish a proper subject–subject association between the two participants. A real dialogue presupposes a clear understanding of the relationship between the teacher, the counsellor and the teaching (the subject matter of the counselling process).

We confess that there is a great risk to be run at this point of our becoming totally idealistic and utopian. Will the strategy as described to this point have any chance whatsoever of withstanding the test of reality? Aren't there too many factors working against it, such as the lack of suitably qualified counsellors or the submissive role of the teacher being counselled, which is due to a long-lasting socialization, and so on? Certainly it can be admitted that it is a strategy which is demanding in many ways. But, on th other hand, to change or adjust existing practice a potent theory such as this is needed. Only then will it give firm direction to change. So, if we think the strategy is a good one, it is surely worth while to continue searching for ways of implementing it.

What is practice?

The emphasis so far on the practical theory of teachers as the focal point for counselling, as opposed to their teaching practice, may give the impression that this kind of counselling takes place in a purely theoretical sphere and will therefore be of interest more to theoreticians than to practising teachers. In the end the prime concern of the teacher is always: What am I going to *do*? Løvlie (1974), in an article on educational philosophy for practising teachers, and in another on the meaning of 'practice' (1972), has helped us clarify our position on this point. He illustrates the character of educational practice in the form of a triangle divided into three levels:

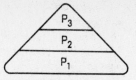

Figure 2.1
The Practice Triangle

The P_1 level is the level of manifest *action*. This is where we operate when we walk into our classrooms and explain, ask questions, give assignments, motivate, evaluate or whatever. At the P_2 level, however, we are at a 'conceptual' level of *planning and reflection*. When I prepare myself for what I am going to do — thinking and wondering about how to do it, looking for ideas within my knowledge and experience, searching for guidance for decisions about what to do, as well as when I review what I have been doing today or recently, trying to see what I can learn from it — then I wander around at the P_2 level. The P_3 level, finally, is the level of *ethical consideration*, where I find myself at times. Here I reflect in another mode, asking myself (and others) whether the way I teach is right or ethically or politically justifiable.

P_1 level: Take Mrs Howard for instance, the German teacher. She practices teaching German in her own individual way every year. When the term starts, she gives the pupils their daily homework of German grammar, then checks carefully every day to see whether they have really learnt what they were assigned. Those have not done the work properly (and there are always some, as you know, who for different reasons have not) she makes a fool of them publicly in front of the class, in an ironic way, trying to make them feel embarrassed. In other words she 'puts them down' before the very eyes of their class-mates. And this is repeated until nobody will risk coming to her classes unprepared in German grammar.

P_2 level: The reason for this practice is that Mrs Howard has found from earlier experience that this is a method that really works. She has tried it out and refined it over the years. Besides, she has also found that there is good evidence in psychology that the social motive of peer-approval is a very strong one, particularly in pupils of secondary age; so she knows that her own practical experience has some scientific support. She has also found that those of her pupils who really do their grammar homework pass, with very good results, the kind of examination that is traditionally given. Some of them, however, whom she has met later on in their lives, complain that they did not feel competent in practical communication in German when they actually had to use the language.

P_3 level: In a discussion at a meeting in the German department at her school, she is questioned by some of her colleagues as to whether her practice could be considered ethically justifiable or not. They thought that it was not acceptable to treat pupils in the above way; that it was, at least, not in accordance with central values expressed in the aims of the school. Mrs Howard did not agree with this and referred to the effectiveness of the method. On the other hand, she said, she did often wonder whether it was right to put such a heavy emphasis on the formal aspect of German, but did so because the external examinations emphasized such knowledge. Certainly there was evidence that most of her pupils would need a mastery of practical language skills for the purposes of daily communication. She had, however, thought it right to give priority to the minority who needed good marks in the examination in order to be accepted at university.

From this example it should be possible to see that restricting the concept of *practice* to the P_1 level only — that is to what actually happens in the teaching situation — is an undue limitation of the scope of our concern with teaching practice. What actually happens must be understood and eventually questioned just as much at the P_2 and P_3 levels — in other words at the levels of what we have called the practical theory of the teacher. We therefore consider it essential that counselling with teachers be so arranged that all three levels of the triangle of practice are included in the discussion between the practising teacher and the counsellor.

A closer look at the kind of arguments that may occur at the P_2 and P_3 levels may further clarify our understanding and lead to the provision of a better background for analysis in the counselling session, both for teacher and counsellor. Again we lean on the terminology and analysis of Løvlie.

Plans or prescriptions for teaching practice, whether they are merely thought up by teachers on their way to school or found at leisure in extensive methodologies of teaching, consist in principle of what Løvlie calls 'practical statements'. Practical statements contain recommendations for educational practice in the form: 'If you want to achieve this and that, then you ought to do so and so.' Or they can be put in the personal form: 'As I want to achieve this, then I shall do it this way'. The form of such statements will in practice vary considerably. They may be lengthy paragraphs stating the results which one might be aiming at together with pages full of description of how to go about achieving these results. In principle, however, they follow the form above. In addition to this, both the individual teacher (at least when questioned about it) and the writer of the book on methods will give reasons and justifications for the practical statements included in the plans and prescriptions. These reasons will be of different kinds, and Løvlie suggests the following categories:

Theory-based reasons: These are reasons which refer to *theory* or empirical results which have been established by research. In the example featuring Mrs Howard, there is a reliance on this kind of reason when she refers to motivation theory and to knowledge from developmental psychology. Evaluation of reasons of this kind must, of course, be made in relation to the scientific criterion of *truth*. Is it really like this? Does the theory refer to conditions in reality and is this reality comparable to the one in which we are teaching? Even so, as we have already seen, educational research offers competing truths which are both controversial and tentative and is, accordingly, questionable as the sole basis for action.

Practice-based reasons: These reasons are those that refer to practical evidence about what *works* in teaching. The criterion referred to here is not truth but *applicability* or *effectiveness* in practice. Mrs Howard knows from experience that her method works, and will probably also be able to refer to colleagues who can support her observations. Whether she could find evidence in research or theory to support it or not would not alter the fact that the practice has proved to be appropriate. Confronted with 'practical statements', the teacher will not only have to test their value in terms of their scientific truth. She must also evaluate them against the criterion of applicability. If someone suggests that groups of pupils with a high level of anxiety in test situations ought to be grouped separately in different classes and taught differently from pupils who are low on this trait, the teacher will not only (or perhaps not even primarily) be interested in checking this recommendation against theories about motivation and anxiety. She will, rather, have to consider if this is a practical suggestion that has a fair chance of working when confronted with all the other conditions which have to be considered when grouping procedures are established. On the other hand, when testing the 'practical statement' in this way against the criterion of applicability (looking for practice-based reasons from her own or other people's experience), she does not take into consideration the important ethical aspects of the problem. This is done, however, when it comes to the so-called 'ethical/political justification.'

Ethical/political justifications: At this point, we have to consider what are the *ethical* implications of the 'practical statement' in order to establish a basis for decisions of a *moral* nature. Mrs Howard is asked to give justifications of this kind for her practice at the meeting in her department, and is confronted with arguments from her colleagues which indicate a conflict between different values. At this point, Mrs Howard fails to appreciate what kind of justification is being asked for and supports her action with reference to her practice-based reason: it has proved effective. This is something which we often do, because we are not sufficiently aware of the distinctions between the different categories of argument described above. It is thus important to make these distinctions clear in order to improve the teacher's conscious refinement of her own practical theory; and, accordingly, it is something which ought to be emphasized in counselling with teachers.

Summary

So we can end the excursion into the concepts and clarifications adopted from Løvlie. Returning to the concept of a practical theory, we can try to summarize it in the following illustration:

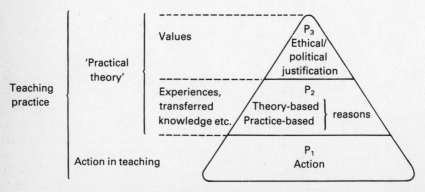

Figure 2.2
Relationship between practice and practical theory

Teaching practice is more than what actually goes on in the direct encounter between pupils, content and teacher. It also includes the planning and evaluation activity which comes before and after this encounter, and refers both to the actions of teaching and to the underlying practical theory of the teacher concerned. Initially, we subdivided this practical theory into three components: (1) Personal experience; (2) transmitted knowledge and experiences; (3) values. In the language of Løvlie, represented here through the triangle of practice, we have found that 'practical statements' (recommendations for educational practice) may be supported by reference to two levels of reasoning:

— practice-based and theory-based reasons, which is but another way of categorizing what we have called personal experience and transmitted knowledge, and so on, and
— justifications based on moral/ethical/political considerations, or on what we have referred to as values.

The illustration above is, however, lacking in one important respect. It may give the impression of a freedom of action/which we have already denied. A number of *frame factors* (resources, localities, material, rule systems, structures, and so on) — impose restrictions on the 'free choice' of the teacher (but also offer possibilities!). These factors also influence the way experiences and knowledge are perceived and thus actively 'distort' the reflections on which we base our practice.

After this rather long excursion into a series of explanations of the pre-conditions for the thesis presented at the beginning of this chapter, we may return to the thesis itself to see if it has now been better established and whether it carries more meaning at this stage than it did when it was first presented. There may, at the very least, be a better basis now for accepting or rejecting it, or for putting it to the test of practical experience.

Notice what we have actually been doing during the preceding discussion:

— we have tried to establish *theory-based* as well as *practice-based* reasons or evidence for the thesis;
— we have, as well, tried to establish ethical/political *justifications* for it, based on value statements relating to education.

In order to give yourself personal experience in carrying out an analysis of such an argument, and thereby to make it more meaningful to you, try to go back and analyse the chapter in the terms given above (and elaborated in the previous section). Which of the given reasons and justifications do you find sufficiently well established, and which of them fail to satisfy your standards? What are *your* reasons for your conclusions? Put your analysis to others to get their reactions. Does the analysis help you — at least — to clarify your own practical theory for counselling with teachers, even if it differs from ours to some extent? What have you planned to do to clarify and expand it further?

Then go back to focus on *thesis*:   Every teacher possesses a 'practical theory' of teaching which is subjectively *the* strongest determining factor in her educational practice. Counselling with teachers must consequently originate in each teacher's practical theory, seeking to foster its conscious articulation and aiming to elaborate it and make it susceptible to change.

3

Counselling in Practice

In chapter 2 we tried to identify the main purposes and functions of counselling in order to establish a sound theoretical basis for our practical procedures. The next task is to describe these procedures that are to be adopted to ensure that counselling in practice really fosters each teacher's practical theory, develops independence and responsibility and stimulates change and growth.

The ideas behind a strategy are important, and their value depends upon the extent to which the practical arrangements devised to implement them do, in fact, ensure the intended process. However, before we dive into considerations about counselling in practice, some comments are necessary.

We suspect that some readers will concentrate on the technical practical arrangements described and regard the 'speculations' presented so far as of little interest and importance. If the main interest of the reader is in searching for recipes, however, the central point of the strategy may easily be overlooked or poorly understood. To us, it is the line of reasoning presented in Chapter 2 that really matters. So, we insistently refer to the description of what takes place in counselling sessions as a conceptual *strategy*, not as a *method* to be followed in a detailed, step-by-step manner. All of us who are engaged in counselling try to improve our methods and practices in order to come closer to what we would really like to achieve. When the ideals are clear — and kept in sight in all the practical details of the work — we might be able to improve many of our counselling practices, including the strategy proposed here.

What will be dealt with in this chapter are the practical arrangements we have developed as *our* way. The focus will be on the *counselling document* and on the *steps in a counselling session*. The content of the counselling document will contain concepts that for the most part are familiar to people working in the field of education.

The description of the counselling document, as well as the steps involved, is restricted to *one* counselling session. However, counselling with teachers usually takes place over a period of time and consists of several sessions. In teacher-training, a counsellor — the supervising tutor — usually has the responsibility for a *group* of teacher-students for a certain period of time. In consultancy work, the counselling process extends as long as is agreed by the qualified teacher and their counsellor. In any day-to-day co-operation between colleagues, mutual counselling ought to occur frequently and play a natural part in their interaction. Therefore, it would be misleading if our focus on individual sessions were to be regarded as indicating the scope of the entire process in all circumstances.

A counsellor has to consider counselling to be an unfinished, progressive processes. Initially, the major concern will naturally have to be with establishing a good and adequate relationship. An important part of this is to make the strategy explicit and a matter of concern to both participants. Other matters are given higher priority later on (for example, the amount of confrontation in the situation might increase). There will also be a progression from the easier aspects of a teacher's work to the more difficult, personal aspects.

The content dealt with in counselling will also be different, to some extent, during different phases of the process. At the beginning, much attention will need to be paid to the teacher's practical theory, to make it both conscious to the teacher and known to the counsellor, so that it is possible to focus on the development of it. Training in teaching skills and methods might be given closer attention later on, when it is possible to identify which of these each teacher has a wish or need to improve.

The counselling document is an important part of our strategy and it is regarded as a key element in the whole process. However, it is time-consuming to prepare and to apply. Consequently, it is not appropriate to demand the preparation of one for each session the teacher is teaching. When a teacher or student-teacher is working full-time it may be applied in two or three lessons during the week. It is important, though, to establish a pattern of working out documents throughout the counselling process as a regular part of the work. In due course, the way of working as a teacher and the way of relating to teaching — and to counselling — that is aspired to in the counselling strategy will, we hope, become more or less habitual. When this happens, the document itself becomes superfluous.

The counselling document is usually prepared by the 'counsellee' and describes the plans for a teaching session. In the beginning a teacher will often need help to prepare it, if it is to be a useful tool. Perhaps more importantly, she will need experiences that show the document to be a really important product — something worthwhile to be worked out in detail. In an early phase of the counselling process, her documents will often be incomplete. Still, considerable attention must be paid to them by the counsellor.

The counsellor too has *his* ideas and plans for *his* teaching as well as *his* counselling. When *he* prepares a document of the same kind for some of his teaching sessions, this might help the teacher both to experience the process value of it and to become acquainted with the counsellor's practical theory of teaching. We consequently urge counsellors (and teachers in educational theory in teacher-training institutions) to undertake the same kind of work as they will expect later on from teachers or student teachers. It is essential, too, to expose his own documents to the same critical attention and discussion as will focus on those of the 'counsellees' later on.

This point leads us to a reminder. Counselling is only a *part* of teacher-training. It is not correct to consider counselling as able to take over the role of theoretical studies. It is necessary to acquire much theoretical knowledge to become a skilful teacher. This is done mainly outside the counselling process. It is the *application* of theoretical knowledge that provides the content of counselling.

It is a most difficult task if one aspires to apply, and show the relevance of, *all* theoretical content in a teacher-training programme. On the other hand, teaching practice itself might live its own life, apart from any theories, in a very reduced and restricted way. When this is the case, it is usually at least partly due to organizational factors, for example the fact that different persons have responsibility for theory and practice.

However, counselling related to teaching practice may have other functions than the mere application of theory. Through practice the teacher may gain a fresh perspective on and approach to theory, a richer understanding of it, and, perhaps most importantly, the realisation of a need to read more.

Educational theory may indeed be very theoretical and live *its* own life. Productive counselling generates a need to know more, a need to study the literature in order to become a better teacher. Our principal focus is on the teacher's practical theory of teaching. *Her* theory *is* already an integration of practical and theoretical elements (in a traditional meaning of the word 'theoretical'). *Her* theory needs input from both sources. This is what counselling is about.

Now to the strategy itself. We have thought it best to present the practical aspects of counselling fairly early in the book. In Chapter 4 and 5 we will elaborate further on the principles involved and on the content of counselling sessions. We hope that, in this way, we will have shared a common understanding of possible practical arrangements with you before we go into further details of the principles involved.

The counselling document

A counselling document is intended to be a detailed account of a teacher's plans for a teaching session or a teaching unit. It is prepared in advance and discussed with the counsellor (and, ideally, also with other participating teachers) in two steps. We will return to the steps later on. Before that, we have to make a brief run-through of some concepts applied in the document, mainly to give meaning to what we have called 'process-intentions'.

Teacher intentions and realities of teaching

When analysing a teaching session, it is useful to distinguish between what the teacher has planned to occur and what the teaching actually turns out to be. Teacher intentions are seldom expressed clearly. They are not always made explicit to the teacher but are more like general ideas about what kind of activities should take place what kind of materials should be dealt with or what content should be covered. Sometimes objectives are clearly stated and/or a schedule is made up.

Teaching situations differ as to how much the teacher can decide for herself and how much is left to others (superiors, colleagues, students) to decide. In most cases a lot of decisions are self made.

In restrospect one can judge if the teaching session turned out as planned. (It might, of course, turn out quite differently.) An important way through which we, as teachers, gain experience is by comparing and reflecting upon disparities between pre-made intentions and teaching realities. (The importance of this comparison in evaluation is pointed out strongly by Stake (1967).)

It must be added that rather different opinions exist as to how thoroughly teaching sessions ought to the planned for. There are, of course, dangers involved in thorough planning (rigidity, inflexible teacher behaviour, scarce allowance for student influence) as there are when planning is deficient or completely absent. Even minimal planning may be advantageous, giving opportunities for creativity, commitment and involvement.

Why, what and how

According to Scandinavian terminology (here translated into English), *purpose* is the term applied for that which one is trying to achieve by educational measures. One speaks about the purpose of an eductional system, a discipline within the system or even within a smaller part such as a lesson. The purpose is generally stated in broader and vaguer terms when referring to larger sectors of an educational system than is the case for smaller elements. Usually the teacher is obliged to conform to more or less generally stated purposes, although differences exist from country to country and from one educational level to another. Officially stated purposes have, of course, to be interpreted and made more specific by the teacher.

Purpose relates to plans, to *why* teaching is considered to be an adequate measure. When analysing whether teaching in fact has produced the intended or other outcomes, one is dealing with what are regarded as the *functions* of teaching. Function relates to teaching reality as purpose relates to teacher intention.

To achieve the purpose, one has to have some notion of what the students are supposed to learn in order to conclude (in retrospect) whether the teaching contributed towards the fulfilment of the purpose or not. The knowledge, attitudes and skills that should be established fall under the usual headings of *aims* or *objectives*.

It is common to experience difficulty in distinguishing the terms 'purpose' and 'objective' from each other in practice. It might be helpful to think about what kind of discussion typically goes on (with yourself or with others) in relation to each of them. If the discussion is mainly dealing with questions as to *why* content, methods, and so on, should be used, you are discussing the purpose. If, on the other hand, you are concerned with what qualities, understanding, experience, and so on, you would like the students to have or develop, you are discussing the objectives.

The terms presented so far are probably familiar to most of you. In addition to the more familiar terms, however, we find it useful to introduce Thomsen's term *'process-intentions'* (1975). The term has direct relevance to the practical theory discussed previously. 'Process-intentions' are intended to be an operationalization of a teachers' practical theory as it is applied in one specific situation. The question which process-intentions are supposed to answer is *how* the teacher will perform a teaching task when purpose, objectives, student characteristics, and so on, have been identified. (We should like to add at this point that this statement is definitely not meant to imply that purpose and objectives are always to be decided upon before the teacher meets his students. It often happens that decisions on this point constitute a major element *within* the teaching process, as a matter to be argued about and decided upon collectively.)

Process-intentions are fairly detailed accounts of a teacher's intended plans as regards activities, materials, methods, roles and so on. They might be called descriptions of the intended teacher *strategy* (as this term is used, for instance, by Nielsen 1977). Making explicit process-intentions means thinking beyond the teaching methods one plans to apply. It does not mean abandoning talk in terms of methods, but rather that the further task for the teacher is to spell out how all the elements of practical theory are to be applied in a specific setting.

The preparation and application of process-intentions in counselling means applying what we think of as a 'telescopic' view of the preparation of a teaching session — an in-depth approach. It is certainly not an easy task to write process-intentions. We are not usually accustomed to this kind of detailed planning, to this kind of explicitness and outspokenness. Student-teachers are even less so. However, it is most important to have this kind of detailed account available in counselling.

Writing out process-intentions in advance is a sensible thing to do in other respects as well. Pre-made intentions, concerns and reflections are, in fact, unstable. It is not enough to rely on memory. After the event it is very difficult to recollect one's thinking without severe distortions from what has in fact taken place.

From the counsellor's point of view, it is essential to have the teacher's intentions written down, making it possible to relate intentions to realities. From the teacher's point of view it might be regarded as a trap; what is requested could be seen as an attempt to expose inferior planning so that it is easy to be critical afterwards. However, when the counselling strategy is made fully explicit, displaying process-intentions is likely to be regarded very differently by the teacher. As one wrote: 'It is better if you can explain your lesson before the supervisor begins to criticize, because it sounds like an alibi after that' (Lewis and Miel 1972, p. 220).

The content of the counselling document

The 'telescopic' approach to teaching and counselling may lead to a focus on detail and a consequent loss of perspective. A single lesson is almost always part of a total program and should be regarded as such. A large part of the counselling document should therefore deal with the relationship between the single unit and the whole from which it is extracted. Process-intentions will reflect this relationship, focusing on the illustrative character of the single unit as well as on the peculiarities of the unit itself.

The layout of the document could be that proposed by Thomsen (1975):

1. *The nature of the session.*
   This means giving a sketch of the teaching unit, the program of which it is a part and the characteristics of the content, students, materials, facilities and so forth. Any special conditions of the session should also be given.
2. *Purpose and aims.*
   (a)   The teacher is requested to refer to the purpose of the total unit from which the session is taken (if such overall statements are given) and her own interpretation of that purpose as well as of the single session.

(b) Subsequently, information is needed on the aims of the total unit, whether given by others or whether the teacher has decided upon them herself.

It is advisable for the teachers to present aims/objectives for the single session. They should at the very least be precise enough to give information about the relative weight given to knowledge, attitudes and skills and about the level of knowledge (judged according to some texonomy of educational objectives) which is being established.

When objectives are to be decided upon by the teacher and pupils together, the frames within which decisions *may* be taken should be made quite explicit.

3. *Schedule for the lession.*

A brief outline is given of the activities that are to take place, possibly with approximate time estimates.

4. *Process-intentions.*

This is the main part of the document. It is recommended that as detailed a description as possible about the following aspects be given:

— What the students/pupils are to do.

Learning is a consequence of activity. The teacher should state what kind of learning activity, that is, what kind of behaviour the students are to engage in. Does the teacher intend to have active, responsible students? Are the students to be listening, performing, arguing, reading or what? *How* exactly are the students to work with the content of the lesson?

— What experiences would the teacher like students/pupils to have? The teacher may want them to have certain experiences for various reasons. It may be, partly, that there is reason to believe that objectives can only be reached in this way. It way be that some experiences have their own special kind of value. Or her reasons may be concerned with concomitant learning that has to be balanced against concern for the explicit objectives. The teacher is asked to give as detailed account as possible of what kind of experience the students are to have.

— What kind of 'climate' does she aspire to 'produce'? What intentions are there as to the 'tone' or 'emotional quality' she wants to generate in the session? What kind of inter-personal relationship does she aspire to establish? Is the climate to be cooperative, competitive, production-oriented or aimed at being emotionally secured?

— What is the teacher to do?

When the other aspects of the process-intentions have been decided, the objective is to state what kind of teacher role and teacher behaviour the situation will require. What will be her major responsibilities (e.g., to inform/organize/support/give feedback)? What will be the teacher's own role, complementary to the role(s) out-lined for the pupils? What does the teacher consider to be appropriate behaviour?

This is one way of editing a counselling document. Usually, it covers from one to three pages.

As regards the editing of the process-intentions, it may vary considerably. In some cases, a detailed description of the 'climate' may be essential because this aspect is considered to be the most critical factor in the lesson. When this is the case, extensive consideration about this aspect should be made. In other cases, the role pattern between the pupils and between the teacher and pupils may be more extensively elaborated. This may be done by paying much attention to student roles which, to some extent, also define the role of the teacher; or vice versa.

Writing process-intentions might turn out as the expression of more or less wishful thinking. The teacher may easily be lead to express idealistic conceptions about how the lesson would be if, in a pertinent phrase, 'all mankind was good and the weather was nice'. On the other hand, the extent of this wishful thinking may be somewhat reduced by the skilled counsellor. In any case, any tendency to overlook realities will be inevitably counteracted during an extended counselling process. After all, over-idealistic conceptions will become visible to the teacher at a later stage, when process intentions are related to teaching realities.

Before turning to the description of an example of the counselling procedure, we would like to remind the reader that counselling with practising teachers is done under quite different circumstances. Some teachers seek, or at least welcome, the opportunity to get feedback on their teaching. In some cases the reason is simply that they have no educational training whatsoever. (In Norway, as in Britain, you will not normally get a position as a teacher without educational training, except in a university or in further education). In other cases, they may have come to that point in their teaching career when they feel need for renewal and inspiration. Whatever the reason might be, it is evident that the task of a counsellor is quite different in a situation where the student teacher has to attend in order to become qualified, compared to that in which counselling is actively sought by an already-qualified teacher.

Our belief is that there exist counselling strategies that can be profitably applied in a variety of counselling settings. We invite the reader to judge the applicability of the proposed strategy and, more important, the applicability of the principles of counselling to the setting(s) he is familiar with. Perhaps you will find that our proposals necessitate changes in the practical arrangements found within your institution. If that is the case, please judge whether your practical arrangements *have to* be the way they are before you conclude that our strategies and principles are wrong. For a discussion of counselling principles see Chapter 4; and for their application, Chapter 6.

As mentioned before, we invite the reader to share our strategy of counselling and, later on, to take part in a discussion as to which principles are important in counselling with teachers. The order of presentation of the strategy is quite intentional. We feel that a discussion of principles can easily become too abstract if the frame of reference is not related to counselling practice.

Three phases in counselling

Usually, supervision and counselling with teachers takes place primarily (and often exclusively) *after* the teaching unit is finished. Counselling is rare before the teaching commences; that is, it is normally restricted to a brief run-through of a general plan or schedule. Counselling of this type is clearly incomplete. Our example of a strategy consists of three steps, each with its own distinct purpose and characteristics.

It is usually most beneficial to counsel on the basis of normal teaching situations, i.e. by letting the process in the teacher's own classes be the focus. It can be done for units of a single or a few lessons, but it is usually more effective when it is possible to encompass larger teaching sequences.

A second choice is to prepare artificial situations in which the teacher performs with participants other than ordinary pupils (e.g. with other teachers as pupils). In these cases, the content has to be selected with the artifical character of the session in mind. Although this arrangement is a second choice, in our experience counselling on how to teach can in fact be carried out quite successfully this way. In Chapter 6 we discuss the application of our counselling strategy to different settings, one being this type of artificial setting.

Under all circumstances, our strategy rests on the assumption that educational processes which are dealt with in counselling can be broken down into teaching units. In natural settings, a teaching unit often corresponds to a lesson from the class schedule. In artificial situations, one is free to decide upon the size and complexity of a teaching unit.

When focusing on teaching units, as we do, there is a danger involved that the perspective of the counselling might become narrow and that some of the fundamental issues involved are excluded. We like to think of teaching units as examples of general educational situations and educational problems. One of the counsellor's major tasks is in fact, to shift the focus from details to generalizations. This view reflects a belief in learning principles which stress the value of digging deep in cases that are chosen as representative of many others. How much may be lost in this way we do not know, but we are more afraid of the superficiality which comes from considering many cases rather than the limitation which the idiosyncracies of a few cases presents. The phases involved in the strategy are as follows:

The Initial Phase

Teachers with whom counselling is carried on have to be made familiar with the concepts and terms applied, particularly the concept of 'process-intentions', and they must be given opportunities to prepare counselling documents for themselves.

In a situation where students in teacher training go out on teaching practice, the selection of content and the form of the teaching unit are both clearly limited by the need for continuity in the program already devised for the classes they attend. Even here there are, however, some possibilities for selecting ways of teaching which correspond to the interests of the student teacher.

During the initial step, the teacher and the counsellor should reach a general understanding of how to arrange the teaching as well as the counselling situation. Ideally, the expectations of both teacher and the counsellor as to the nature and aims of their interaction should be made explicit, discussed and adjusted to fit each other. It is usually necessary to spend much time on the clarification of counselling purposes and functions. At the very least the teacher should realize the existence and value of practical theory; and the necessity to make it 'visible' both to teacher and counsellor.

How much time and effort should be spent on the initial phase obviously has to be decided with reference to the specific situation. However, placing too little emphasis on it may later turn out to be a serious drawback.

After the initial phase, each participant writes down a draft for the counselling document for one unit. The document(s) produced by the participant(s) are the main materials for the next step. As suggested earlier, the counsellor includes in this phase the production, discussion and implementation of such a document by himself, as an example, setting the stage for further activities by the teacher(s).

Pre-teaching Counselling

The teacher's plan, as it is expressed in the counselling document, provides the starting point for the pre-teaching phase.

The perspective adopted in this phase is purely hypothetical. The plan is discussed with its assumptions and justifications. One looks into the possibilities of succeeding with it. The focus is not entirely restricted to this single unit, as the unit is more or less taken to be an example of similar teaching units. The intention is to have an exchange of experiences, of value perspectives, of knowledge etc. that might have relevance to the teacher's plan.

The counsellor's task is, among other things, to pay attention to the internal consistency of the plan, posing questions about the relationship between situational characteristics, purpose, objectives and process-intentions in order to help the teacher elaborate and improve it. Questions like these might be posed for common reflection and comment:

> Are there other aspects of the situation, which we haven't considered, that it might be important to identify? Are the pupils competent to work this way when they have had little previous experience with it? Is there an adequate procedure for handing out materials without losing more time than necessary?
>
> Are the objectives clear? Is the cognitive, the affective or the psycho-motor aspect the most important? Are the objectives to be determined in advance or should they be more or less open until they are discussed with the pupils? Are the objectives in accordance with long term aims?
>
> Are there reasons to believe that the suggested manner of asking questions will allow the students to 'discover' solutions or principles? Is the task presented to the pupils of a kind that makes group work productive or will it lead to individual work after all? How will the students experience this way of teaching? Might the approach lead to learning that is considered to be inappropriate?

The content of a pre-teaching counselling session will vary considerably from person to person. However, the two main purposes of this session should not be lost sight of:

1. To identify as much as possible of each teacher's practical theory — in its theoretical, experiential as well as its value aspects.
2. To perform a didactical analysis of the teaching unit, helping the teacher to achieve a clearer understanding of how the unit might be carried out.

Teachers should ideally experience the session as being conducted in a relaxed manner by people who are genuinely interested in their way of thinking about educational problems. It should be noted that the counsellor can hardly put on an interested face if he, in fact, has no real interest in the topics of the dialogue or, for that matter, in the teacher as a person.

In spite of the counsellor's intentions of having a relaxed, friendly and co-operative dialogue, his pre-teaching sessions may take the form of a cross-examination. At least that is how the session might be experienced by the teacher. Undoubtedly the teacher will find the discussion difficult and, in some cases, exhausting. It requires some professional skill on the counsellor's part to find a proper balance between cross-examination and indulgence. It is equally important for the counsellor to take the individuality of teachers into consideration; in some cases *support* is more strongly required than intricate questioning — and vice versa.

It is to be expected that some teachers more than others will want to know what the counsellor requires them to do rather than to take a personal stand, and they accordingly will welcome any advice they can get from the 'expert'. In principle, the counsellor should be careful not to comply too readily with any such expectations. On the other hand, total reluctance to offer advice might easily be experienced by the teacher as contrary to the counsellor's role as an interested helper.

Ideally the pre-teaching session should not take place within tight time limits. There should be opportunity to reflect. Consequently, the issues dealt with should invite such reflection; and the counsellor should be careful not to give answers that reveal his conclusions on matters that the teacher might benefit from by dealing with personally.

After the pre-teaching counselling, the teacher may revise the counselling document *but not just to comply with ideas presented by the counsellor*. It is this uncritical assent to the wishes of the counsellor that we particularly want to counteract.

Post-teaching Counselling

Post-teaching counselling should ideally take place immediately after the teaching unit. In a course setting, everyone who participated in the teaching unit should also take part in the counselling. In normal settings, it is both a practical as well as an ethical question whether pupils should take part or not. The ethical problems involved relate both to pupil-integrity as well as to the integrity of the teacher involved. It is our conviction, however, that the possibility of having at least some colleagues participate in counselling sessions should be exploited. (A discussion about counselling in groups is presented in Chapter 6).

When equipment is available, it may be of some help to have the teaching unit recorded (on audio or video tape). The teacher may (and usually will) find it useful to observe their own teaching behaviour.

Simple video feedback is, however, not the most important aspect of its use as far as counselling is concerned. Recordings offer the possibility of checking what actually happened at crucial points — points which are variously perceived or interpreted. Recordings may also reveal dimensions of the teaching unit which were not apparent to the participants during the session. Analyzing deep-level aspects of a teaching session requires, however, plenty of time for analyzing the recording and this may conflict with the need for immediate post-teaching counselling. It should be remembered that video feedback is not at all a necessity for adequate counselling, and its importance should not be overestimated. In a course setting, we advise participating teachers to watch the video recording of their teaching in private or together with the colleagues they would like to bring along.

Counselling on the basis of a careful analysis of video recordings can profitably be utilized in a counselling program in separate sessions following some time after the immediate post-teaching session.

The perspective in the post-teaching sessions is, of course, no longer hypothetical. Whether a teacher has access to a counsellor or not, it is an important step within educational practice to evaluate her own teaching by relating intentions to realities. In a counselling process, it is the counsellor's main task to assist in the teacher's own reflections on teaching practice. Two categories of questions may be concentrated upon:

1. How did the teaching unit turn out, compared to what was intended? What emerged differently from what was intended and why did it turn out that way?
2. What consequences may be drawn, on the basis of the experience gained, as to the relevance of the plan as a whole as well as of the crucial stages in it? What were the lessons learnt that may relate to other teaching tasks or to education in general? What were the contributions of the experiences to the practical theory of the teacher?

Both categories of questions ought to be represented in post-teaching sessions — not in strict order, but in a natural way. Questions such as the following might be considered during post-teaching sessions:

Was the plan carried out as it was planned? Was it the right thing to do or should it have been adjusted or even been put aside? Did the teacher succeed in playing the part intended? Was the behaviour of the pupils as intended? Did they *really* behave as intended or do we just imagine so because that was what we expected of them? Was the climate established close to what it was intended to be? What about the realism of objectives, content, student characteristics etc?

When discussing whether the objectives became a reality or not, one is easily seduced into believing that the pupils did learn what they were expected to learn. Consequently, however difficult this is to ascertain and touchy to ask about, it may be worthwhile to reflect upon what we actually *know* about student learning as against what we *suppose* about it.

The actual performance of the teacher should be related to her intentions, both as they are documented in what she has written and as the counsellor has become familiar with them during the pre-teaching session. Any 'short-comings' should not be judged by absolute standards or criteria but as consequences of intentions implemented during the particular teaching unit. Inadequate teacher behaviour is certainly not an immutable personality trait but behaviour that is changeable when it is tried out and found to be inappropriate.

The teacher will usually need some assistance in finding out what the teaching unit offers (what is worth working on, what may be elaborated further, what could be worth trying out in further detail, what should be changed, etc.)

At this point, the relevance of having counselling documents prepared should be apparent. The criteria for evaluating the teaching unit have their origin here. In this way some pitfalls may be avoided. Without the documents and the previous session, the practical theory of the *counsellor* is the most evident and immediate source from which criteria can be deduced; and, usually, the process of deduction, as well as the theory from which deduction are made, are not really open to challenge by the teacher. The criteria applied may therefore come to be considered as absolute and definite, as *the* criteria for what is 'good' or 'correct' teaching. The teacher involved can very easily come to regard the counsellor's criteria in this way instead of achieving a measure of independence in the situation.

The relevance of having an analytically potent terminology as a tool in analyzing teaching events should be apparent at this stage. In our strategy, anchoring points for the discussion with the teacher are to be found in what the teacher has said in the counselling documents about puroses and aims. The discussion will naturally revolve around the problem of finding and applying adequate means in order to effect the intended outcomes. It is the internal relationships between purposes, aims, frames, student characteristics, content, teaching methods, evaluation etc — as well as their justification — that should be the vital issues in the discussion. (See further about this in Chapter 5.)

At this stage we have to repeat one point from a previous section. *The criteria applied in post-teaching counselling are primarily the ones provided by the teacher herself.* Does this mean that whatever the teacher wants to achieve, whatever plans have been prepared and whatever the justifications are for them, the counsellor should comply with them? Certainly not. The counselling should *originate* in the teacher's own intentions and her actual performance should be compared to what the teacher would like to achieve. However, the teacher's intentions — and the criteria deduced from them — are made the object of a counselling dialogue. What are the justifications for the teacher's intentions? Do we hold the same concerns, the same intentions? In what respects do we differ and what is it that makes us think differently?

A word of comfort for the teacher or student teacher: a counselling strategy involving the application of process-intentions secures the teacher the right to have the counselling focused on the issues which are considered to be important. From time to time, you may have been subjected to counsellors who hold quite different views to yourself. What usually happens in such instances, is that you reluctantly and unwillingly do what you think the counsellor would like, saying to yourself: it is quite wrong, in my view, but what else can I do?

With the help of process-intentions, you do not have to comply with whatever the counsellor wants. Then, at least, the burden of proof is shared, not just placed upon you. He, too, has to justify his suggestions; or you may both decide to give the suggested plan a try and let the empirical test — the test of experience — decide the matter.

As regards student teachers, their concern about certification usually implies an even more pronounced need for having the counselling — and grading — based on process-intentions. It is otherwise possible to receive a low grade mainly because you and the counsellor(s) hold conflicting values or differ in othe respects. It is much harder for a counsellor (either a student's tutor or a teacher taking students for teaching practice) to give you a low grade on the basis solely of his personal criteria when, in fact, you have stated extensively and consistently a reasonable teaching strategy dervied from an explicit practical theory and been able to implement it with obvious success.

Counselling documents should not be considered, however, as a weapon in a battle between teachers and their counsellors. The most important concern to both participants is, of course, to improve teaching. If you, as a teacher, should by any chance consider a counselling strategy similar to the one presented here to be beneficial to your need to improving your teaching competence, but are subjected to a different strategy, it might be an idea worth considering to write down your process-intentions and to ask the counsellor to help you in improving them (before teaching) as well as to refer to them during the evaluation afterwards. This might be helpful to both of you.

Counselling documents can certainly be used as weapons in a battle as well as tools in a peaceful situation. They may also be regarded as are nuclear weapons by the super-powers: their sheer existence is assumed to prevent war! Anyway, if they can be applied in peaceful co-operation to enhance the chances of reaching common goals, that is, of course, much to be preferred. At least supplying them at all means that the match (if there has to be one) is, as it were, played on the home field of the teacher.

Pre-teaching and post-teaching counselling compared

We have noticed differences as to purpose and content between pre-teaching and post-teaching sessions. How the two phases relate to each other may be summed up in the figure below.

Pre-teaching counselling is purely hypothetical and is a discussion of intentions for a specific teaching task together with their assumptions and their justifications. Post-teaching counselling is based upon a tryout and aims at identifying experiences and principles that might have consequences for subsequent trials as well as for the practical theory of the teacher.

Goldhammer *et al.* (1980) advocate a final phase in the counselling process, namely an evaluation of the process itself. We do not want to reject the idea but would like to return to the issues, involved later on (see pp. 67–72).

Process-intentions for counselling

Counselling is itself educational activity — a form of teaching. It should therefore be possible to spell out process-intentions for counselling too. Up to now we have

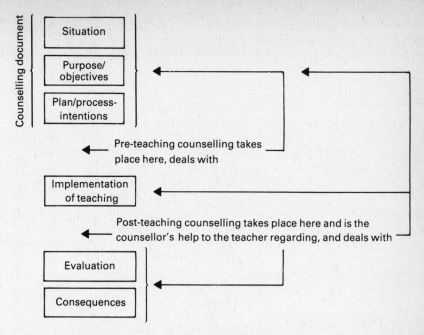

Figure 3.1
Pre- and post session counselling

illustrated how a draft of process intentions can be applied within teaching units to become a focus for counselling. Now we will try to apply the same draft model to the counselling process itself, both to give another illustration of its use and at the same time to be more specific about some characteristics of the counselling process as we conceive it. The first part of what follows takes the form of a more general spelling-out of process-intentions for counselling, while the second part contains an example in the shape of a specific situation.

These are *our* intentions. We don't expect you to agree fully with them. On the contrary, we would welcome a critical rejection of particulars with which you disagree as well as any adjustments and amendments. However, we hope that the spelling-out of our intentions will at least serve as an example to make it easier for you to identify your own intentions for counselling, whether they bear any resemblance to ours or not. Would it be an idea — perhaps at this moment, before reading on — to write down your own process-intentions for the type of counselling activity *you* would like to advocate?

Here are some of the questions we will try to answer in our attempt: What purposes do we have in our counselling? Which aims do we consider to be important? How do we intend to arrange the counselling in order to bring about the intended outcomes? What kind of unintended effects may our counselling practice have; and how should we try to avoid detrimental effects? Generally in this section we will have to be quite brief.

In order to understand the reasons which underlie our various points, we must refer you to Chapter 2 as well as to the following chapters, which may be regarded as a brief representation of our practical theory of counselling.

General Statements

The purpose of counselling with teachers may be stated at different levels. On a very general level, the purpose is to prepare students for the teaching profession or to assist in the professional development of practising teachers. On a more specific level, the purpose has to be based on an analysis of both present and future qualifications for teachers, with reference to the demands of specific school systems or more general demands. The forecasting of future needs is of course a difficult but *important endeavour*. Nevertheless, we have to make our assumptions on what we think our society — as well as the educational system within it — will look like in years to come. However, we don't merely want to adopt our strategies blindly to anticipated societal demands. We have to ask ourselves: what kind of teachers will be able to contribute to the development of our society in a desirable direction?

The general conceptions of intended teacher competencies, identified in the analysis of purposes, will need to be given meaning in terms of *objectives*. What are the important aspects of knowledge, attitudes and skills in teaching competence? Our own general stand in this respect (not related to specific parts of the educational system) can be stated as follows:

> We want teachers to possess a coherent, explicit and relevant practical theory as a basis for their decision-making and performance in their teaching practice. The theory should reflect their basic values and consist of relevant knowledge and experiences. They should have a high level of consciousness about their theory and be inclined to subject it to empirical tests and revisions, as well as to ideological analysis and reflection. They should feel compelled to apply their theory in their daily, professional activity, to reflect upon it and to relate new experiences to their existing theory.

Although it is misleading to conceive objectives as either cognitive, attitudinal or related to skills, it is appropriate to think of these three as different *aspects* of the objectives.

Perhaps in contrast to popular opinion, we consider the attitudinal aspect to be of the greatest importance. In fact, we consider responsibility, commitment, independence and critical consciousness to be vital parts of teacher competence, supported by a mastery of subject content, knowledge of educationally-relevant matters and teaching skills — not vice versa.

We would like to make one reservation at this point. When it becomes necessary for a teacher to improve some technical skill (to apply methods, materials, handle technical equipment etc.), the counsellor should not be in any way reluctant to offer appropriate help. The point is, however, that help in technical matters (which is often the prime concern of a teacher) should be directed towards filling gaps in the *teacher's* practical theory rather than merely demonstrating the counsellor's theory. Otherwise, the teacher may easily get the impression that — in spite of all efforts to the contrary — it really is the counsellor's theory that matters and the one which she ought to comply with.

Process-intentions for counselling have, of course, to be adopted to the specific situations in which they are to apply. However, some general guidelines may be given.

— What is the teacher to do?

We want the teacher to reveal her own theory and to act in accordance with it; to reflect upon it as well as expand and modify it to become a more powerful tool for teaching. We also want to relate any relevant knowledge the teacher otherwise has. We intend the teacher to take, subsequently, an active and responsible role.

We know that the counselling situation might be experienced as stressful and that resistance may show itself before the teacher really adopts this active and responsible role. The teacher should write out her PI's in advance and eventually revise them on the basis of pre-teaching counselling.

— What experiences would we like the teacher to have?

It has been said that teaching is a success when pupils can say afterwards: 'We did it ourselves'. The same holds for counselling. Success is important. Directing one's own teaching practice along unknown paths is a risky business. Unless a certain degree of satisfaction is thereby achieved, willingness to experiment and change established practice diminishes. Practising unfamiliar teaching methods is not likely to be successful without support. The teacher should rely upon the counsellor's help to avoid pitfalls. The teacher should also be made to realize that there is much to learn from so-called 'failures' if they are analyzed and reconsidered. A teacher who implements teaching units that do not work is likely to reach a depressing conclusion: it is not worth trying anything unfamiliar; it won't work anyway. If the counselling is restricted to just a few teaching units, therefore, a reasonable degree of satisfaction by the teacher's own performance is crucial.

— What kind of a 'climate' do we want to be predominant in the counselling sessions?

The intended role pattern mentioned earlier can only be established on a basis of mutual understanding that is reached by a frankness in the essential dialogue. In addition to what we have prescribed for the counsellor, he must constantly exhibit role behaviour that underlines his part as a genuinely interested helper.

The interaction between counsellor and teacher should ideally, be a dialogue on educational matters based on examples that are familiar to those involved — a dialogue that is stimulating to the counsellor as well as to the teacher(s). The dialogue should be one of wondering and reflection. It should explore the nature of the processes involved and seek tentative solutions to the problems encountered. The focus of it should not be so much on the more personal problems of the teacher as on the processes and problems involved — processes which are more or less equally experienced by others who teach.

— What is the counsellor to do?

The counsellor should act as an interested helper, not as the only one to be doing the thinking and bringing solutions to the problems encountered. On the other hand, he should not be completely reluctant to offer advice. The advice, however, should be given as tentative suggestions for the teachers to reflect upon herself, not as authoritative statements which the teacher would feel obliged to accept without question.

We wish to make the teacher understand the role pattern that we try to establish an invitation to either accept it or adjust it. Later on, we want to do our best to act ourselves in accordance with the role delineated for counsellors. In essence, the counsellor's strategy should be one that makes the teacher think for herself, persuades her to find solutions on her own and enables her to become confident enough to draw her own inferences and predict the consequences of her thinking.

When disagreement arises between the teacher and the counsellor (why shouldn't they disagree?), it is important to make it a constructive one. In fact, we *do* disagree on educational issues. Often, it is a mere matter of apparent difference of opinion, arising from different uses of language. In such cases, the disagreement can be overcome in a rational way. Real conflict of viewpoint, however, should not be avoided in counselling situations. We should all learn to accept conflicting positions in education, because they reflect differences in values, experiences and knowledge; and we are bound to learn much about teaching by testing such conflicting views. Counselling sequences which last some time with no conflicting views in sight usually imply a lack of depth in the discussion or a failure on the part of the counsellor to have the teacher's clarification of their own theory to themselves and to their counsellor.

The advice given by the counsellor might profitably consist of alternative procedures between which the teacher can decide, relying on self-reasoning and not on the assumption that one of them is to be preferred because it comes from the counsellor. The principal reason for this expansion is the teachers' need to have their store of methods expanded. With a counsellor available, opportunities are more favourable for gaining direct experience with alternative methods than is the case in daily work alone. The counsellor should read the PI's carefully and discuss them with the teacher, aiming at clarification, so that they can be used profitably for evaluation in the post-teaching counselling.

As you will recall, process-intentions are relevant to specific situations only. The attempt above to make a general case therefore suffers, it will be seen, from obvious deficiencies.

A Specific Example

An example may be more enlightening in illustrating what process-intentions for counselling may look like.

> Mrs Kerbin holds a combined position as teacher in a secondary school and as a tutor in a teacher institution. She is going to have three students visiting her secondary class in biology for a period of three weeks.
> She has had students from the teachers' college visit her class before. She has already met two of the students who are coming this time; David, who had objected to the application of a grading scale with more than two levels (pass–fail) for teaching practice at an initial meeting at the college; and Peter, whom she had spoken with during a break on the same day and who had told her that he didn't really want to become a teacher but was attending the college as a kind of unemployment insurance. The third student is a girl, Susan, whom she has not met. Mrs Kerbin writes out a draft of a counselling document when preparing for their first meeting. She will later ask the student teachers to make their own counselling documents for one or two lessons and so wishes to do the same herself, related to the first counselling session. At the same time, she intends to use her own document as a basis for evaluation after the first meeting.

> 1. *Purpose of the first meeting*
>   (a) Have their expectations as well as my own for the counselling in biology teaching made explicit; and reach a preliminary agreement on the role pattern involved. Make clear what is negotiable and what I shall insist on. State my reasons for this.
>   (b) I want to inform them about some characteristics of biology teaching.
>   (c) I want to inform them about the group of pupils they will be working with, in particular about one or two of them.

2. *Objectives for the first meeting*

I want the student teachers to reflect upon their own expectations for counselling; and to understand how and why I want them to become involved in deciding how we shall arrange our work co-operatively within the frames that I impose. I hope that our meeting will be stimulating and will to a certain degree make them keen to participate. I want to give them some essential knowledge about biology teaching and the class they will be working with.

3. *Process-intentions*

— What the student teachers are to do.

I will expect counter-arguments and objections from the students (and hope to appreciate them so far as they are not totally negative). They should state their disagreements or reservations quite plainly, but not in a way that closes the possibility of argument and discussion. From what I know so far about the teacher students, this might be difficult to obtain. David's point of view on the marking issue was not welcomed at the previous meeting at the college, which perhaps made him more antagonistic and tense than he would have been. In Peter's case, I suspect that he wants to find the easiest way through the college without getting more involved than necessary. I would guess that exposing his own viewpoint and opinions is no part of his strategy. All three of them will need to inform me of their backgrounds and interests to help me become familiar with them as individuals.

— What experiences I would like the students to have.

I want them to experience the relevance of their own reasoning and the importance I attribute to it. I want them to experience the session as a real discussion that matters, not as a chat without significance.

— What kind of 'climate' I want to predominate.

I want the session to be intellectually stimulating and emotionally and socially supporting. I want them to feel that there are demands on them; although it is certainly acceptable to express doubts and uncertainty. The session must not become boring.

— What I want to do.

My main concern is to have the student teachers reveal their points of view. My interest in their expectations and opinions is not a superficial one. I need to know about them; I'm not asking for the sake of asking.

I expect them to be somewhat reluctant and I will, subsequently, have to give them some time when I ask each one individually about aspects of their practical theory which I suspect to be of major concern to them. I cannot expect them to become involved in decisions about the future role pattern if I am not careful to welcome their suggestions and objections and prepared to accept the consequences of suggestions that might be presented.

I will try to be fairly specific about which constraints (frames) I do expect them to accept, making it clear what it is that can be decided upon during our meeting. I will try to present the arguments that make it so important (for me?) to have them accept these frames.

I will try to conduct the meeting by focusing on issues that are considered important by me or assumed to be important to them. However, any concern for a strict order is definitely subordinate to the over-riding concern for allowing the student teachers to experience a high degree of participation.

As regards my personal behaviour, I want to be frank and honest, being careful not to give any reasons for my suggestions, points of view or the frames imposed that are irrelevant or superficial. I want to appear friendly, considerate and interested — with a reflective attitude towards my work.

These are the process-intentions of Mrs Kervin. Afterwards she performs a brief evaluation of the session.

It had turned out to be difficult to have the session in accordance with her plans. David had insisted on reviving the discussion about the grading systems at the college, claiming that a discussion about counselling without reference to the grades was irrelevant. Peter was not interested in 'abstract principles of counselling', as he called it, but was eager to know now many lessons each of them would have to teach, what content areas they would have to cover and so on. He asked if it was possible to choose one topic himself. He would very much like to teach about pollution problems in rivers and lakes in a particular region of the country. Susan repeatedly referred to the teaching principles and preferences of other counsellors she had visited so far, obviously trying to get an impression of the preferences of Mrs Kerbin.

Mrs Kerbin got a strong impression during the meeting that the student teachers were unwilling or unable to make explicit their own preferences and, even more so, the reasons or convictions underlying them. They were skilful in identifying the preferences of their counsellors. They were, however, applying rather broad categories in their judgment of counsellors. Some were modern, some were old-fashioned, some were concerned about order and quietness in the classroom, some about pupil interest and activity, some about orderliness of presentation and so on. She realized that it would be even more difficult to establish the role pattern relevant to her counselling strategy than she had expected.

It became obvious that the student teachers had become accustomed to a situation in which they were exposed to counsellors with different teaching styles and where they had no real possibility of having differences in the counsellors' teaching preferences explained and discussed. They had evidently rarely experienced any real freedom to explore their own ideas and preferences. To benefit from her way of counselling, the student teachers would need to be retrained; but the possibilities for doing so were limited. After all, they would only stay in her classes for a few weeks. But at least she could do one thing: if all the teachers engaged in counselling the same students could come together and discuss their counselling, they could probably make a little progress. She decided to call such a meeting. Mrs Kerbin also decided that David would be the first to teach. He, more than the others, could probably find his own way and be able to present some reasons to back his teaching. She would expect some disagreements, but hoped that her way of approaching differences of viewpoint would have an encouraging effect on the other two. They might then realize that disagreements on educational issues are to be expected and do not, in fact, represent threats either to themselves or to the counsellor.

Summing up

At the end of this chapter, we would like to make a few comments which may improve your understanding of the text. We have, over and over again, stated our conviction that every counsellor should make his own practical theory explicit to himself so that he can eventually inform others (for instance teachers) about it, in cases where clarification would be beneficial in one way or another. The same principle applies to the writing of this book. We (speaking as authors) have *our* theories of teaching (which, in fact, are not as close to each other as this text may imply) as well as our theories about counselling.

Is it possible for you to decide, on the basis of the text so far, about any similarity between your theory of teaching (and of counselling) and the one presented here? In what respects do your points of view differ from ours? What do you think might explain the disagreements: differences as to values, knowledge or experience? Does your theory imply other strategies for counselling than the one we present? If so, in what respects?

4

Basic Principles Underlying the Counselling Strategy

In this chapter we will — on the basis now established — present a number of principles which we think are important to grasp if the basic ideas of the counselling strategy are to be implemented. As indicated before, we think that these principles are indeed more important for the quality of the counselling than the concrete procedures that we have followed and which we have described in Chapter 3.

Before presenting the principles, however, we want to offer a negative stipulation for counselling by describing briefly an important criterion which should *not* occur in the kind of counselling we advocate. We do this by returning to the strange little animal we introduced in the preface of this book.

In counselling practice we may often, with regret, realize that teachers have adopted what we characterized as the strategy of a chameleon: that is, they figure out the preferences of the counsellor and comply with them, without any personal conviction or commitment. For reasons which we have given in Chapter 2, we hold this to be a wholly detrimental effect of a certain kind of counselling and, therefore, one which must be avoided.

There are obvious reasons for a student teacher adopting this chameleon strategy. If she is subjected to the advice of several counsellors, she soon learns that each counsellor has different preferences and concerns with regard to teaching. One counsellor is often not aware of the nature of the practical theories of his colleagues — and for that matter the nature of his own theory. The criteria applied are likely therefore to differ from one counsellor to another and the differences between the criteria will remain unexplained and unjustified. With the student need for certification in mind — as well as her wish to receive as good a grade as possible for teaching competence — the chameleon strategy is clearly an expedient one from her point of view — at least in the short time perspective.

A major concern for the counsellor is, therefore, to make counselling operate in such a way as to free the teacher to go *beyond the chameleon response*. The teacher should, of course, be helped to see that she is in fact using this passive strategy and to understand its limitations. The counsellor and teacher together might search for situational elements which would foster a more liberating strategy. Still, it would be idealistic to expect the teacher to pay the obvious price when circumstances make the chameleon strategy the most immediately profitable one, with respect to certification and grading, no matter how inappropriate it may be in a longer perspective. Accordingly, it is up to the counsellor to establish counselling situations in which the chameleon strategy is not profitable. Otherwise we risk what Dewey (1904) says, that:

> immediate skill may be got at the cost of power to go on growing (p. 15).

The precedence of the teacher's 'practical theory'

In our way of thinking about counselling, we are primarily concerned with the actual 'practical theory' of the teacher — both as a starting point for counselling and as the entity that has to be further elaborated and developed in order eventually to revise practice. It is the teacher herself who is the only person who can change this theory. All that others can do is to influence it, create situations which may favour or hinder change and provide input which may *eventually* lead to change. This changing — or rather this remodelling, restructuring, expansion or consolidation — of the theory is a personal thing which can only be done by the teacher herself. We do not at all imply by this that nothing matters in counselling because the teacher changes or not according to her own will. On the contrary: what goes on in counselling does make a definite difference. But the change — the new content and structure of the theory — is ultimately due only to the teacher concerned. On the other hand, it must be noted that there are certainly limits to the practical possibilities of a (changed) practical theory. Many ways of teaching that the teacher would like to implement, based on her existing knowledge, understanding and values, are not realistic in practice — for instance, those that clash with frame factors which it is not up to her alone to control.

Due to our prime insistence on this point, you may have noticed that we always refer to the process we are discussing as counselling *with* teachers. To us this means that counselling is a process where people get together to question, analyze, experience, evaluate and experiment with ways of teaching in order to develop further their understanding of and ability to act wisely in teaching situations. The process is one where a teacher does this *with* a counsellor in order to develop her teaching, and not one where the counsellor leads this development or change in certain, pre-established directions. Nor does the counsellor prescribe concrete methods/procedures for the teacher to follow, supervising the implementation of these. Consequently we are not dealing with the counselling *of* and supervision *of* teachers in relation to a supposed right way of teaching. We are dealing with counselling *with* teachers in order to help *them* develop *their* way of teaching and a well-established, conscious basis for it.

Counselling for independence

Comparing the amount of time during which a teacher has access to formal counselling (in a strict sense of the word) with the long span of her professional career when she is largely left on her own — or, at the most, in the supportive company of her colleagues — gives an interesting perspective on counselling. Effective use of this limited part of a career must, from the very first moment, aim at developing in the teacher an independence which is based on a realistic conception of what she can do and why she wants to do it. This independence must be accompanied by a tendency to continue to develop both her teaching practice and her underlying theory, preferably in continued co-operation with others. Counselling must establish a model for the essential activity we want the teacher to continue to practice all through her vocational life: theory-based planning, observation of and reflection upon her own practice, use of her own experiences as well as evidence from others — all these should come together in a constant effort to develop and refine a consistent practical theory as a basis for further plans and practice.

We believe that this description of a teacher — one who is using experience systematically as a basis for continued development — corresponds quite closely to the ideas presented by Stenhouse (1975) about 'the teacher as a researcher' and we would like readers to follow his argument on this point.

If this practical ideal of a teacher is going to prevail — at least to some extent — it is imperative that the counselling situation be one in which the spiral relationship between theory and action can be practised and experienced as successful. We cannot implement a counselling practice in which we tell people how to behave and then expect them to be independent and self-propelling as soon as they are left on their own.

Counselling must accordingly try to foster independence, not in such a way that teachers will no longer need help and guidance but in a way that will induce them to seek it when relevant (from their colleagues, from literature and from other people), as a natural part of their professional work. The teacher must learn both to take responsibility for her practice as well as to be unhappy with any superficial or 'once-and-for-ever' basis for it.

The exemplary* character of the teaching which underlies counselling

In teacher training, one important requirement is for the teacher to be given practice — to be offered experience in practical situations, to learn what it is like, how it feels, what the problems are, what she can do and what she needs to master etc. These practical teaching units, in which the teacher performs in her professional role and where the counsellor (and eventually other student teachers) are present, furnish *examples of teaching situations* which are shared by those present. As such they are useful illustrations of what teaching can be. They also have the advantage over situations which the different participants in the counselling relationship have experienced individually and apart from each other that they give a *shared experience*. They are thus excellent starting points for discussions about and

---

*'Exemplary' is here not meant to connote that the quality of this teaching is outstanding and is to be taken as an example to be copied. It refers merely to the fact that the teaching is an *illustrative example* of an important phenomenon which may thus be made the focal point of discussion and reflection.

analysis of teaching (in general). Counselling, in fact, is about teaching in its great variety of forms, not only about the particular unit of teaching just experienced. The latter is only one small sample of a large 'population' of teaching units which the particular teacher will offer. To limit counselling to an evaluation of the teacher's performance in this particular situation is to reduce unduly the potential of counselling. On the other hand, counselling must start with what took place or was planned in the particular situation, using this as an instance of teaching from which analysis and deliberation can be generated — aiming the whole time at transfer from this to other teaching-learning situations. This is, in fact, to focus on the underlying theory of the teacher, making the particular teaching an experience from which something can be learnt which is useful in other — even quite different — cases. The controlling idea is to look for the general in the particular.

Let us take an example. It is the beginning of the school year in the first form at Greenhill Secondary School. I am visiting Janet — as her counsellor — who is there on practice in Miss Lee's class, teaching history. I follow her teaching for a lesson in which she is dealing with the American War of Independence. She has come to the point in the development of the conflict where the war breaks out and wants first to review what has happened up to that time, to establish the background of the war. She does this by asking the pupils questions to see how much they are able to recall of the content they have been dealing with so far. This is fully in line with her process-intentions, which she has given to me and which she has previously discussed with Miss Lee. These do not, however, say anything about the character of the questions, indicating only her intentions to activate the memory and understanding of the pupils as far as the background and reasons for the war are concerned, and to spread the questions around the class in order to involve all pupils.

In the course of this part of the lesson, however, it strikes me that all the answers she gets consist of only a few words which are shot back at her from the pupils who are answering. Certainly she manages nicely to draw in most of the pupils in a natural way, avoiding making the questioning into an examination — clearly in line with her intentions. Still there is something peculiar about the whole activity. I begin to wonder whether the pupils themselves would be able to construct and formulate any kind of coherent description of the background for the war, or if they are only able to fill in short bits of factual information in 'blank areas' in Janet's questions. Is *she* really establishing the connection between elements in the background of the war by means of the sequence and content of her questions, while *they* are only providing bits of information on the basis of 'signal-words' in her questions? If this is to some extent correct, what is the reason for it?

In the post-teaching counselling, where the three of us are talking about the teaching unit we have just experienced, I bring up my observation after a little while. Janet had not noticed this limitation of her mode of questioning during the lesson, but recognizes it when she looks back on what happened. Miss Lee had not reacted to it this time, but says that the same thing had struck her earlier in some other classes. Janet wonders if this may have something to do with what we encourage pupils to regard as knowledge in schools, referring to her own experience at school where factual information (names, years, sizes, numbers etc.) predominated, as against connections and possible (not to say conflicting) explanations etc. I point out that we often run the risk of supporting this conception in pupils of what is valuable knowledge, because we are ourselves caught out by the kind of response we get from them. They, again, have been trained to respond in this limited manner: so, we continue to ask the kind of question which leads exactly to that kind of answer. The risk is always there, not only as far as types of questions and answers are concerned, but in all aspects of teaching. Miss Lee contributes to the topic by telling the story of how she had once realized that she was conforming to the 'set' of a class where no one volunteered to ask questions themselves but only responded to questions asked by the teacher. This passed unnoticed by her until it was pointed out by a colleague who was teaching in the same class. She then had to start a deliberate 'campaign' in her class to change this pattern of behavior so that it would be more consistent with her real notion of the place of questions in teaching.

In the course of the session, this phenomenon came right into the foreground of our discussion. It was related to role theory and the idea of complementary roles, the school as a socializing agency which produces results different from those formally intended and the difference between intentions and functions in teaching. We also discussed the relationship between types of questions, assignments and tasks used in teaching and the taxonomic level of the learning resulting from it; as well as the more fundamental question about whether such implicit functions of teaching (not contained in the explicit educational aims) are in the interest of the existing society and are thus fulfiling important societal functions of the school.

Janet's teaching certainly leads to this discussion, but it would not have done if we had restricted ourselves to merely describing and evaluating what happened in the lesson. Of course, we might have noticed the type of answers given by the pupils and said to Janet: 'You distributed the questions very well among the pupils, but try making them answer in full sentences instead of just single words.' But this would hardly have led us into giving the background in relation to which each of us offered Janet advice; and she would have added just one more method to the repertoire of overt behaviour at her disposal rather than building up her practical theory. In the event, the session ended by Janet proclaiming that she found this to be an important weakness for her to do something positive about. We then discussed possible alternatives for her process-intentions for a series of new lessons in which she would like to discuss this matter with the pupils to try and help them change their response-pattern (as well as her pattern of questions). This would be likely to make them more aware of the connections and explanations behind what they read, and better able to formulate these in their own language. She would also try leaving it more to the pupils to ask questions and to help each other by suggesting answers to them.

End of the example: back to the principle! We have tried to illustrate that, by looking upon the shared units of teaching as *examples*, we can be lead into productive discussions about teaching, aimed at increasing our understanding of, and creativity in it. Rather than being constrained by what happened and even by discussing how it ought to have been, we are freed to use our collective experience as a starting point for even wider excursions into the field of teaching and education.

Two reservations: first, there are of course good reasons why much that we talk about in both pre-teaching and post-teaching counselling is very closely related to process-intentions and the actual teaching reality. This will often be of such immediate interest to all the participants that it would be foolish not to focus on it. We ought, however, to feel free from time to time both to 'magnify' some apparent 'detail' in the play (a good illustrative analogy for certain things found in teaching) and then to make that the focal point of our deliberations while putting it into a wider perspective of theory and experience.

The other reservation concerns the teacher's perspective and interests. What is made the centre of interest in the counselling session has to be central to the teacher and not just a consuming interest of the counsellor. Prolonged talking about some detail which the counsellor finds absorbing, but which the teacher in question finds neither challenging nor even interesting, has no chance of influencing in the slightest the teacher's practical theory. Any point for discussion has somehow to be related to the concerns of the teacher, either by reference to what is or what, from her point of view, on reflection, *ought* to have been included in her thinking about the process-intentions.

Beside the effects already mentioned of regarding teaching practice as illustrative, we think that this attitude may also lead to a stronger focus on what happened in the teaching period rather than on the teacher as a person. It is the teach*ing* as example and subject-matter that we must focus upon for our learning, not the teach*er* as a person to be evaluated and judged. This may help in creating a matter-of-fact attitude towards the teaching where, as it were, some 'distance' can be combined with 'concern' as a professional.

In conclusion: the type of counselling used in both sessions should not have as its ideal a full coverage of everything that happened (the so-called wall-to-wall version) but should rather use *parts* of what happened — those parts experienced as central by the teacher, taken as examples which may be expanded to form a starting point for excursions into the field of teaching and education in general.

Counselling as 'discourse'

Throughout most of the text above, you will find that reference to the communication between teacher(s) and counsellor in counselling situations is referred to as 'discussion'. Our experience has been that this terminology creates misunderstandings from time to time. The term 'discussion' will, for some, have the connotation of a 'debate' where different points of view confront each other and where there is argument on the basis of different opinions. A debate is by definition something which is carried on between participants who are in opposition to each other. This type of situation is not implied in our use of the term discussion. To us, discussion has some of the associations of the term '*discourse*'; that is, it means a thorough discussion and investigation of a defined phenomenon (for instance the use of a specific method of teaching in a given situation) where the aim is *not to win* the debate but to understand more fully.

Henriksen (1978), much in the same tradition, defines education as a 'power-free dialogue' where the aim is to pursue further understanding, with none of the participants exerting power over the others throughout the process, and where the better argument gets the priority.

At the beginning of many counselling relationships you may find that the teacher acts as if she were defending herself against attacks from the counsellor. The relationship takes on elements of the 'why-don't-we-yes-but' game that people play at times. To almost any comment by the counsellor, the teacher's type of response will be: 'If you say that, then my defence will be . . .' In our experience, it is important to make this attitude itself a topic for discussion. In other words, communication is needed about the character of the counselling relationship.

In a real discourse the *subject matter* itself is the important element, not the persons participating in it. They may take on different roles from time to time —

sometimes questioning, at other times trying to explain, to be critical, to evaluate and to suggest new 'solutions'. The main aim is to *become wiser together about the subject matter concerned*, to disclose differences of view with the reasons for them and to analyze likely explanations and solutions as to their possible effects etc.

This attitude of 'together we look into a shared problem' which characterizes a real discourse is not always easy to establish, particularly in relationships where roles are not typically perceived as being on an equal footing. Establishing it is accordingly a process where explicit communication about it is vital. At the same time it is a fragile attitude or relationship where rather small signals — particularly from the counsellor — may suffice to ruin it. Double-communication in this area is easily registered by the teacher, and the verbal message is quickly over-ridden by the message communicated by other channels.

Counselling does not automatically develop into a discourse. This quality of counselling has to be *actively created* and is vulnerable because of its exposure to lots of threats against it. To a large extent it is more of an ideal, than a reality — still an ideal to be pursued. Efforts of establishing and maintaining counselling as a discourse is primarily the responsibility of the counsellor, although this responsibility must eventually by be shared the teachers during the course of the counselling period.

Counselling as confrontation or prop

Two caricatures of counselling exist in practice and may be used to illuminate the point we are trying to make here. Sometimes we find counsellors who are so eager to support the teacher in order to 'build her up', to be positive and not destructive in their counselling, that they have virtually nothing to say about the teaching witnessed, except that it was so good. There may be a minor detail, of course, that might have been better handled, but this is so marginal that it is hardly worthy of notice. (There are counsellors who *start* like this, but who follow their tolerant introduction by a list of such 'details' so long that it is sufficient to put down the strongest teacher).

On the other hand, a different kind of counsellor has almost nothing positive to say about the teaching or the teacher but states a number of objections, points out scores of mistakes and presents a generally negative attitude which implies that there is hardly any reason to believe that the teacher will ever be able to teach properly.

Most counselling fortunately falls between these two extremes. The strategy of counselling that we present may run the risk of ending at either of these two poles if it is not properly understood and practised. As we are pleading that counselling should start from the intentions of the teacher and use them as criteria for evaluation and further counselling, we certainly run the risk of being totally accepting of anything the teacher wants to do, confining ourselves to checking whether she succeeds in carrying it out in practice. This may lead us into total permissiveness and an inappropriately positive attitude which is in fact often humiliating to the teacher concerned, as it clearly shows that the counsellor does not take the teacher seriously.

On the other hand, we also argue that the counsellor should help the teacher to

disclose the theory behind her actions and that he should probe for such a theory in the counselling sessions. This may just as easily lead an inquisitive, negative attitude on the part of the counsellor, where anything the teacher suggests or does is regarded by him with the utmost suspicion as to what might be its underlying motivation.

As we have said a couple of times already, teaching is an activity where the practitioner is exposed and vulnerable. Put in a counselling situation you — as a teacher — are wide open. For this situation to be fruitful for the teacher support is needed from the counsellor. We have already indicated the importance of the climate in counselling sessions as a means to this end. The teacher must feel safe to try out things, to make suggestions, to make her views known, to disagree, etc. She must feel the genuine *support* of the counsellor when she is trying to master the problems of teaching, even when she is going about it in a different way from that probably favoured by the counsellor.

Describing counselling and teaching situations like this, and trying to implement them in practice in accordance with such a description, may lead us into a safe but barren learning situation. The teacher feels free and secure in her practice but is not confronted by the counsellor with any challenges for fear they might disturb her feeling of security. Let us therefore look at counselling from the point of view of one who recognizes the need for *some* kind of *confrontation*.

In order to develop her teaching practice and the theory underlying it, the teacher needs to be presented or confronted with alternatives to her theory and practice — to be to some extent challenged as to its tenability. We have already introduced, as an important element in this counselling strategy, the fact that the intentions of the teacher need to be confronted with what happens in reality when the plan is carried out in the classroom. This is one form of positive confrontation. Even this may, with some teachers, lead to a rejection of what they have experienced in the form of a straight denial of what really happened in class. Through mechanisms of distorted perception and repression, experiences are thus made to conform much more to the expectations and intentions of the teacher. This is a barrier to any productive use of the experience as a basis for change both of theory and practice, and is one of the things counselling should help to overcome.

But even using this type of confrontation with reality, we are operating only within the framework of what the teacher herself has the imagination to think of and carry out. In a learning situation — which counselling with teachers essentially is — the scope or perspective has to be considerably widened. The teacher needs to be confronted with other possibilities as well, both when it comes to practice (methods, arrangements, techniques) and theory (conflicting evidence, alternative experience of others, different values, etc.).

The responsibility for such a confrontation rests with the counsellor. And·it is here that the possibility of what we think of as 'negativism' is particularly strong. If the counsellor persists in introducing alternative methods to those suggested by the teacher, and refers constantly to different theoretical or practical evidence which contradicts what the teacher says, he may be putting a heavy strain on the relationship with her. This situation requires a delicate balance that needs some practice in achieving, as well as constant evaluation from both contributors if it is to be mastered. Our own experience is that we, from time to time, in our over-eager efforts to confront the teacher with alteranatives or arguments for consideration, have ceased being productive counsellors. We have, however, also learnt that in most cases this need not be fatal to the counselling relationship, providing the counsellor is willing and able to notice what is happening and openly admits his failure to act productively.

Consequently, we feel that it is important that an element of confrontation is, again and again, presented in counselling, to provide potential material primarily for the further development of the practical theory and also for an enlargement of the repertoire of techniques and methods used by the teacher. Confrontation must be balanced against the need for the teacher to select and try out (uncoerced and with support) what *she* has decided for herself, in order to create *her* own classroom experiences and thus to provide a basis for the revision or fortification of *her* theory.

Reference to two different forms of learning may at this point throw light upon the point we are trying to make. Piaget (1954) refers to two qualitatively different forms of learning which we apply alternatively in our effort to understand and master the world around us. They are labeled *assimilation* and *accommodation*. In assimilative learning, we gather information and have experiences in order to support and further elaborate the conception and structure we already have in our minds in relation to a specific task, problem or phenomenon. We have, in this way found a way to explain what we observe and to use new experiences to further refine and confirm our knowledge. This is a brick-building activity where new bricks are added to the structure already established.

At intervals, however, we may suddenly be confronted with a situation where our established knowledge does not suffice to explain our observations. We experience bewilderment and have to search for a new structuring of our knowledge which can cater for the new experience — we utilize, in a word, accommodative learning. This means that we have to break up the framework previously established to re-establish what we know in a new way. This may take time and is certainly a challenging and, to some extent, uncomfortable experience; although it may also contain an element of pleasant, rewarding feelings as the new structure is established. In terms of our allusion to building activity, this accommodative learning is an activity of reconstruction.

Following such accomodative learning activity, the need is felt to try out and refine the new insight gained; and then assimilative learning follows.

An example may illustrate the difference. This one is taken from counselling with practising teachers at a school which is experiencing problems with a lot of noise and unrest in classes. There is a lack of pupil responsibility for their own work, for the property of the school and for each other. The teachers have collectively taken up the problem, and through discussions at teachers' meetings as well as in smaller work groups, they have tried to develop a strategy for changing the situation. They have decided to invite the pupils to take part in discussions about how the situation might be changed, and to make them realize *their* responsibility for the existence of the problem and for suggestions as to how to solve it.

However, the situation following these discussions remains much the same as it was and the pupils refuse, by and large, to accept the responsibility offered them for participating in the change. The teachers, who feel they have presented a thorough line of argument, both of the situation as well as of the measures to be taken, are confused. They call upon a counsellor from the local advisory staff to help them analyse what is happening.

Through observation, participation in teaching sessions, as well as discussions with teachers and pupils, the counsellor develops an understanding of the situation. By means of examples from the life of the school, he tries to show that the invitation to share responsibility, given to the pupils, was limited to this particularly problematic situation which the teachers were unable to cope with themselves. Whereas, in other parts of the life of the school (selection of subject topics to work with, allocation of resources to books and other materials, responsibility for learning activity etc.) they were *not* asked to take any responsibility at all. The reaction of the pupils could probably be more meaningfully understood given this perspective. This understanding might lead to different measures being taken by the teachers in the actual conflict to those tried earlier.

What happened is another story. The point here is that the explanation suggested by the counsellor calls for *accommodative* learning on the part of the teachers — a new understanding, based on a reconstruction of what is already 'known', through the adoption of a new perspective. Assimilative learning is no longer sufficient: accommodation is called for.

Knowledge about these different forms of learning is of importance to the counsellor, as teacher behaviour may be better interpreted and understood with this perspective and as measures may be taken to stimulate the appearance of the different learning forms. For accommodation to occur, there is a need for some challenge to the existing structures of knowledge (or theory) of the teacher or at least for some incompatibility between her knowledge and new experience. It will largely be up to the counsellor to provide input which increases the possibility of such learning taking place at times when it is judged to be beneficial for the teacher. This judgement is a matter of experience as well as of training. Once developed, it allows the alternation between assimilative and accommodative periods of learning to serve as a very useful concept for the counsellor. There are certainly limits to how much of challenge, confrontation and conflict the teacher is able to cope with in an accommodative learning phase; and new structures which have been established through such learning need to be very firmly established and refined for them to really become effective in the practice of the teacher. Assimilative learning is also needed throughout what is a complex process, and the counsellor ought to help in providing situations for this to occur.

There may seem still to be a kind of conflict between support and confrontation in counselling. When challenged and confronted with conflicting alternatives in experience, knowledge and values, your state of mind is usually characterized by a feeling of insecurity. However, we have come to the conclusion, so far, that it is possible to establish a climate of *emotional* and *social* support and security and at the same time introduce an *intellectual* challenge or confrontation. We even think that this is not only a possibility but is, in fact, a precondition for the challenge to the teacher to be productive for her learning. To enter into an accommodative learning phase may be experienced as threatening because you have to give up your firm conception of the world around you. There is reason to believe that this move is more easily ventured upon in an atmosphere of emotional and social security than when the opposite obtains. In our opinion, the counselling therefore ought to take place in a climate where the teacher knows and experiences the counsellor as a caring person — one who takes interest in her and is eager to help and support, as well as to offer ideas, suggestions and evaluation for the benefit of the teacher herself — and not only to parade himself or to exercise his power. In this climate, many more of the counsellor's alternatives or questions will be tolerated and applied by the teacher than in a different atmosphere.

The supportive element in counselling is, however, not only restricted to the emotional and social climate. It is also important in relation to the *practical* core of teaching, in that the counsellor ought to help the teacher in putting her ideas into practice.

Kathy wants to try out an idea she has about letting the pupils in the second form formulate for themselves certain laws or rules in physics on the basis of experiments in class. She bases her ideas on lectures she has attended at the college on the work of Bruner (1960), about which she is quite enthusiastic. As her counsellor, you are very familiar with these ideas and have learnt to apply them to some extent in your classes; but you have learnt from experience that, if you are going to implement them at this level, you really have to have modest aspirations as far as the complexity of the laws that these pupils can formulate is concerned. So, instead of letting Kathy go about it in an unrealistic way which will cause her to experience failure and possible resignation ('Bruner is certainly an interesting fellow but completely useless in practice'), you support her by helping to select suitable laws and experiments which stand some chance of giving a successful result both for the pupils and for Kathy. You discuss her process-intentions at length, helping her to clarify what she is really expecting to happen and whether her plans have any chance of being carried out in the time she has set aside for the teaching. You also remind her to have all the equipment ready for the experiments in order not to waste time or to create confusion, thus distracting the pupils from the central task. In all, Kathy gets the feeling that you are there *with* her, playing your part in the venture to make it as successful as possible. You are not lurking around in the background, knowing a lot beforehand that rules out any possibility of the teaching being a success, without saying a word until, smugly, afterwards you comment: 'Exactly how I thought it would work out. I could have told you so.'

As a counsellor, you are like the safety net or, rather, the coach on the safety rope when the teacher is training for her act high up there under the roof of the tent. But you don't just wait to pick her up when she falls, telling her what she did wrong. You also help her think through her act in advance, offering her your own experience as well as encouraging her to reflect on hers, in order to increase the probability of her making it without the use of the net.

This is also an important rapport to establish as a base for the teacher's further willingness to try, experiment and take part in inovation. If such efforts are connected with positive experiences in the training periods, there is a much greater probability that they will continue in practice. A series of negatively experienced failures during training will probably increase the risk of creating a rigid, frightened teacher whose practice in the future will reflect her fears.

Counselling as critique

The concept of 'criticism' may help our understanding at this point. Lewis & Miel (1972) write about this in an excellent chapter of their book. The analogy is with the criticism of artistic works but, to avoid the negative connotation of the term 'criticism', the French word 'critique' is suggested as a technical term to be used both as a noun and in a verbal sense. Critique used in this way refers to a process of qualified analysis — the pointing out of the crucial parts of a whole and the relating of these to some norm, standard or value. In our context, this norm would be primarily the intentions of the teacher herself. One of the counsellor's tasks is to help the teacher identify what are the major concerns that define the norm that should be applied. Another task is to present other norms with which the norm of the teacher should be confronted. Lewis & Miel comment upon the character of these norms (or criteria) in the following way:

> However, the criteria themselves are subject to criticism and cannot be forced on anyone. The critic will have a listener only if he can convince another that the criteria he urges are just, appropriate and reasonable. 'Criticism is good and sane', wrote Herbert Read, 'when there is a meeting of the artist's 'intention' and the critic's 'appreciation'. (Lewis & Miel 1972, p. 228).

As used within the arts, the term critique refers to a skilful analysis and judgement of the artistic product (or process), performed by a person who is recognized as knowledgeable both in the artistic field and in the process of technical criticism. He expertly measures the works of art against standards of judgment that are widely accepted within the particular tradition to which they belong and not against mere personal likes and dislikes. A well-trained critic is exercising 'connoisseurship' (Eisner 1975), a quality well worth aiming at by any counsellor.

Still, there is an analytical distinction to be made between 'critique' and 'counselling'. It seems to us to lie in the element of 'advice'. The critic takes a position which is completely outside the creative activity of the artist, engaged as he is in analyzing the art-object carefully and in relation to norms or standards. For the counsellor, on the other hand, this 'external' position is necessary not sufficient. He has, in addition, to engage himself in helping the artist (i.e. the teacher) to find alternatives that can be put into practice. He, accordingly (to quote Kwant by Lewis & Miel (p. 231)) to some extent.

> . . . places himself on the side of the object of critique. He does not do this in such a way, however, as to take over the responsibility from the artist/teacher, but by sharing her concern for her future work.

Roles involved in counselling

A role may be defined as the sum of expectations about the behaviour of a person holding a certain position. We expect people around us to behave in accordance with the expectations we have of them in their position. The expectations connected with some roles (pope, king, prime minister, etc.) are strict, but in most roles there is room for variation within an acceptable role performance. As a rule, however, a person playing a role will be accepted by others only to the extent that his behaviour lies within the limits acceptable for that particular role. If it is not, he will be considered unpredictable, unrealiable, etc. and his attempts at co-operation with other people will be made difficult.

In education, a role perspective can often be a powerful analytical tool. It may have strong implications for understanding the interplay between teachers and pupils, teachers and parents, etc., and — which is our concern in this book — between counsellors and teachers.

Some of the roles that may be identified in education are complementary ones; defining one implies — at least partly — the definition of the other. If a teacher more or less deliberately decides on the way she wants to act as a teacher, she is not only defining her own role but is prescribing roles for her pupils as well.

This fact has many implications. An illustration may throw light on one of them. We can take an example from a teaching situation rather than from counselling.

> Mr. Hill has been a teacher for several years and is, for the moment, somewhat dissatisfied with his way of running his classes. He has become increasingly dissatisfied with the way he has been teaching since he started his career, knowing that he has not changed much since then. When offered the possibility of attending a course in one of his subjects (geography), he welcomes the opportunity of having some new ideas to apply later in his classes.

After a tremendously interesting course, he really works hard at changing his plans for the next term. He had expected his students to at least welcome and appreciate his efforts so becomes very depressed when in fact they don't.

By chance, he later on meets the geography professor, responsible for the course, who asks him how things are going. 'Well', Mr. Hill says, 'I don't want to imply that your course was bad. Not at all. But, frankly speaking, the ideas presented, which I thought were brilliant, are not applicable in this school — at least not in my classes. It may be that I got it wrong or that my pupils are not like pupils in general. Anyway, I actually tried but it did not work. It is easy to present new ideas far away from the classroom, but it is a different matter to make them work in school'.

Mr. Hill's reaction is meant to be symptomatic of teachers trying to change their roles. Certainly, ideas that are conceived away from the classroom are sometime's useless for practising teachers. Mr. Hill, therefore, may be correct. Still, there is also the possibility worth considering that the ideas presented in the course were all right but that Mr. Hill's implementation was at fault.

Pupils have limited experience as far as teaching methods are concerned. They get accustomed to the methods of their teachers, be they good or bad. A teacher trying to change the pattern he is used to following cannot automatically rely on his pupils' acceptance. The concomitant changes in the pupil roles represent a move away from the usual, and the probable reactions are confusion, uncertainty and, possibly, rejection.

Counselling, representing again an example of an educational situation, also involves a pair of roles — the roles of counsellor and teacher. Persons holding each of the roles have expectations of their own as well as the other's role behaviour. Generally speaking, both sides are happy with the situation when the other participant conforms to the expectations held. When this is no longer the case, the new role played by the counterpart must be understood and accepted for the role system to work smoothly.

Understanding roles implies, among other things, familiarity with the situation in which role behaviour takes place. It may be worthwhile examining in some detail the roles of the teacher and the counsellor.

Being subjected to counselling — the teacher's role

To have one's own teaching examined is usually an uncomfortable experience. Most of us are not used to having other teachers watching our lessons and the sheer novelty of the situation might explain some of the unease. This is, however, far from the entire explanation.

To teach is, to a certain degree, to reveal some of one's own personality. It is more difficult to behave as intended while teaching than in many other situations in which we put ourselves on view. And we all know it is like that! So, having one's own teaching examined is usually personally very provoking. It is even more so when teaching is something we do not master as well as we would wish, as is often the situation for teachers early in their careers. Among teachers in general, it is rare to find persons who are actually fairly content with the way they teach and who express pride in their work (at least not when colleagues are watching.) This is neither meant to be a generally valid description nor any broad insult, but our experience has given very few examples of successful teachers who have a realistic picture of their own competence and who speak openly about it. Few of them would perform in a teaching session with colleagues watching without to some degree feeling uncomfortable.

Educational situations often contain much unpredictability and uncertainty. They, as we all know, represent fairly complex processes in which we are dealing with other persons (the pupils) who exercise a strong influence on the outcome. Further, we all know that opinions, values and prejudices vary considerably as far as educational matters are concerned. So, judging such situations is a delicate business.

In sum, the teacher subjected to counselling finds herself in an awkward and uncomfortable situation whether she is in training or already qualified. It is common to observe teachers' unease in counselling situations and this is reflected in the language they use when talking about their teaching afterwards with colleagues who have been watching. The feeling of inferiority and vulnerability is reflected in expressions like '. . . when you are accusing me of . . .' (instead of '. . . when you are saying, expressing, etc') then I will defend myself by . . .'

The fact that exposure to counselling is stressful and difficult explains some of its consequences. In order to make the situation more tolerable, the teacher may choose to conform to what she thinks the counsellor thinks — to what he wants her to do or would have done himself in the situation. Then there is not so much at stake, not so much to lose; and this is combined with an increased possibility that the counsellor might approve of what she is doing.

With the teacher focusing on what she thinks the counsellor might approve of, she cannot follow her own practical theory. The theory becomes less important and is felt by her to be inferior to that of the counsellor. The result might we'll be dependence. The teacher becomes, that is, less inclined to follow her own ideas and more dependent on what other persons might say, think or feel.

Such practice leads to conformity. A teacher who tries to escape an uncomfortable situation in this way is not likely to experience any conviction about skills and methods she might otherwise have tried to develop. The teacher's relationship to the knowledge and skill she is practising is likely to be superficial.

What has been said here may seem to be an unduly negative description of what it can mean to be subjected to counselling. Admittedly, counselling does not have to be experienced like this and is certainly not experienced like this in many cases. However, in a situation where a counsellor is not aware of what to avoid and what to look for, our description, however dark and depressing it may seem, is not far from reality.

Hypothetically, it is possible to conceive of a rather different role for the teacher in the counselling situation. Whatever her reasons for seeking counselling may be, a teacher is, for the most part, aware of her strengths and weaknesses; and she may approach the counselling with a wish to get some help to remedy some of these weaknesses. If we can, at this moment, disregard the certification problem (see Chapter 6), it is possible, in theory at least, to conceive of a counselling strategy that takes into consideration each teacher's legitimate right to receive a program that she herself thinks will benefit her teaching. Roles and responsibilities are then changed. Whereas the teacher was the inferior party in the first relationship, in this one it is she who makes the claim: 'If your counselling is not helping me, there is no good reason for me spending time on it'. What kind of roles in counselling do we prefer and encourage? Do we countenance a subordinate role for the teacher? Or would we welcome the teacher making demands on the counsellor?

Being a counsellor

One major counselling strategy imples that the counsellor should act as an expert in teaching; as a person whose major task is to teach *how* to teach — one who possesses the correct answers to any problems encountered. A counsellor adopting a role like this will naturally experience some pressure to produce ready solutions to teaching tasks.

Some counsellors have no alternative conception of their role, although they think it is a very difficult one to perform. Most teachers have a restricted repertoire of teaching methods and this becomes very evident to many of them when they come into contact with a counsellor. We all know the importance of situational variables in education and we would like counselling to reflect this knowledge. Still, an 'external' counsellor rarely possesses the same insight into the situation as the teacher. To give relevant advice related to specific situations is definitely difficult.

What happens is, therefore, often one of two things. In some cases, the counsellor 'escapes into theorizing'. When unable to give situationally adapted advice, he can talk about the principles that are usually applicable, the theory that is *usually* appropriate and so forth. The teacher is left with the problems of relevance and implementation. The truth is that the counselling becomes irrelevant to the needs of the teacher but is patently relevant to the counsellor's own need to conserve his role as an expert.

In other cases, we see an 'escape into methods' instead of theories. The content offered by the counsellor will, in that case, be his personal views on method. Advice based on practice turns out to be fairly general as well, dealing abstractly with the essentials of method as these emerge from the counsellor's own practical implementation of techniques he is familiar with. The teacher is still left with problems of relevance and implementation; perhaps to a lesser extent, but particularly with problems of understanding the relationships between methods, purposes, objectives and process-intentions.

The expectations of a counsellor are partly derived from his own conception of counselling, partly from teachers' expectations and partly from the expectations of others (colleagues, superiors, etc.). The chances are greater that a person will comply with expectations about role behaviour when his role conceptions are vague and unreflected. A counsellor will normally be confronted with the expectation (outspoken or latent) that he is the expert who possesses the competence to decide what is appropriate or correct to do and what is not, Therefore, a counsellor needs to have his intended role worked out pretty clearly for himself, and in relation to the environment, in order to perform his counselling in a way he considers appropriate, particularly if this does not correspond to the expectations towards him of those around.

Combining the roles

Role patterns in teaching are not established out of nothing each term; neither are they easily, without effort, redefined at any time we like. As teachers, counsellors or students we have grown accustomed to what we consider to be 'normal' for the respective roles. Consequently, role patterns are to a certain extent conservative or even old-fashioned.

Among other things, we have often grown accustomed to a dependent and uninformed student role. We cannot easily change our more or less conscious expectations as to how students should behave. And it is not easy for them to redefine their role. When they may have tried to do so earlier, it may have been an attempt met with sanctions that have 'taught them to behave'.

This description may be felt to be exaggerated. The point is, however that whatever role expectations student teachers hold — or counsellors hold of student teachers — these expectations are not only determined by our behaviour in *our* relationship with them. In many cases, therefore, we have to establish new role patterns, often radically different from what is considered to be 'normal'.

Re-definition of roles will, consequently, be no small part of the counselling process. As a counsellor, you have to know that it takes time to re-define and that the way you behave has stronger impact than the words you use! This is not to imply that the role pattern should not be subjected to discussion. But there has to be a close correspondence between what you say and the way you behave. We will deal more with this in the next section.

Talking about role relationship is, however, not sufficient. An agreement (or psychological 'contract') must be reached between the teacher and the counsellor. And it can hardly be expected that any teacher will easily adopt a new role if it is not perceived as profitable to her. For that, too much is at stake. Just remember how reluctant you would be yourself to play the part of the counsellor according to a new role description!

Meta-communication: a tool and a professional standpoint

Among others, Bateson (1972, 1980) and others working within the same tradition (e.g. Watzlawik *et al.* 1967, 1974) have made considerable contributions to the field of communication theory. Some of their concepts have direct relevance to counselling work.

Communication contains the two fundamentally different aspects of *content* and *relationship*. We are always aware of the content; we know that communication is always *about* something. We are, however, not always as aware of the relationship aspect of human communication. Still, communication always contains a definition and re-definition of the relationship between the persons involved. It revolves around questions concerning power, degree of trust, intimacy etc. In some extreme cases, the relationship aspect will be predominant with the content only serving as a medium through which the relationship pattern is esablished.

> Imagine a woman in a subway. She is not a woman 'of the people'. A man who has been drinking too much takes the seat beside her and begins to talk to her. Her communication — with or without words — will probably have one object only, namely to ensure that their relationship remains cold, distant and unfamiliar. The content of what she says has no other significance than to serve as a vehicle for her determined definition of the relationship.

In healthy communication, the relationship is established in a way that is acceptable to those involved. When this is the case, communication can really concentrate on the content. There is no longer a need to define the relationship — through talking about some (irrelevant) content — and the participants are free to focus on what the communication is about.

Now, as a counsellor, you will know that the relationship between the teacher(s) and yourself is not likely to be easily established in a way that necessarily makes the counselling productive. (Nearly everything we have written so far may be considered as relating to problems in the relationship between the counsellor and the teacher). The relationship has to be clarified and accepted before the content of your communication may enter into the foreground. This does not imply that the relationship will have to be perfect before counselling can proceed. Ours is, rather, a negative stipulation and signifies only that, as long as uncertainty and bewilderness concerning the relationship exists, the counselling will continue to deal with *that*, with the content considered to be less important.

This principle has an illustrative value for teaching in general and is something the teachers we counsel ought to become familiar with. Teachers' communication with their pupils also contains this dimension of relationship.

Consequently, the relationship between counsellor and teacher has to be established in order to enable the counsellor to deal with the educational matters that are our principal concern. At the same time, the very process of establishing an acceptable relationship should be made visible to the teachers so that they will become familiar with the principles involved and their relevance to their own professional work.

The relationship and content aspects have relevance to the *meaning* attributed to the separate elements within a communication sequence. The meaning attributed to content statements is given by the context.

> Consider: two 5 years old girls. One of them says: 'I'm your father.' You will not correct her obviously 'false' statement when you realize that the context of the statement is one of play.

The meaning of words used in counselling is also given by the relationship context in which they occur. The counsellor and the teacher should, ideally, experience a common context of a kind that favours productive counselling. Often, personal insecurity on the teacher's (as well as on the counsellor's) behalf, produces an inadequate context.

Consider this: Although I am employed at a university, I also teach on a course for instructors within a trade union. It becomes obvious that one of them is very intimidated by my person/role, showing too much respect due to his restricted contact with university people. How different, then, are the contexts that we will be referring to during our communication? What kind of stereotype do we hold about each other? How would this affect our communication?

It is certainly not a waste of time to work on communications problems in a counselling process. On the contrary, it is indefensible for a real counsellor to accept as sufficient the kind of relationship and context that occurs 'naturally'. What we have to do is to apply what we have called *meta-communication* throughout the entire process.

As the word itself indicates, meta-communication means a constant clarification, definition and re-definition of the nature of the communication and relationship as well as the link between the relationship and the content. At a day to day level, it means that when you experience something as wrong, when it is hard to establish and sustain interactions the way they ought to be, there is but one 'tool' you might resort to.

> Consider: You have been spending much effort on making a teacher understand your counselling strategy so that she will state her own needs and wishes. This is aimed at reaching agreement on the nature of the activity you are both involved in. You hope to have established a sound relationship. Yet, during your first post-teaching session, you realize that the 'why-don't-you-yes-but' — game is being played. Your points of view are met by various defensive statements from the other participant. You then have to take out the recommended tool from your 'tool-box'. That is, you express your opinion abut the nature of the communication, you invite the teacher to share her experiences of it with you and you further invite her to participate in searching for a way to continue the counselling.

There is one important reservation to be made. Applying meta-communication may allow a kind of disguised accusation at a later stage. Certainly the teacher may see it as such. ('I've told you how our counselling relationship was supposed to be. Now you are not complying with the rules we agreed upon!') Doing this kind of thing means making a serious mistake. Meta-communication is supposed to be a mutual sharing of, as it were, 'second order' views *about* the 'ordinary' process of communication in the counselling situation. Its aim is to improve this ordinary communication so that both participant will find it more in line with their own interests and intentions. Besides, it gives an opportunity to learn about communication on the basis of shared experiences. This is a learning activity that is of immense value to everyone involved with education.

When you have created together a counselling 'climate' in which meta-communication occurs naturally and regularly, you have also provided yourselves with a safety valve. When difficulties arise later on, they may then be more easily identified, sorted out and cleared away. Do not forget that a counselling relationship may even need to be terminated because too great differences in values makes it unlikely that continuing the process will be worthwhile. Talking about what makes it so difficult will reduce the strong, negative feelings that would otherwise be generated, because the reasons for the difficulties can be identified without great loss of prestige to either participant.

> Consider: As a counsellor at a university teachers' centre, you meet one of the university teachers for the first time. He has contacted you, expressing a need for help to improve his own teaching. He prepares a lesson that he will be giving to a group of new students. The pre-teaching counselling turns out to be very difficult. He then accepts your invitation to meta-communicate. It transpires that he has no experience as a teacher. Consequently, he is uncertain both as to the professional content as well as the teaching task. You also find out, however, that you in fact hold very different views on a wide range of topics that are very relevant to teaching (democracy, epistomology, politics, power etc.). Together you identify what makes your relationship so difficult; and it is then possible to reach an agreement to end the counselling after having shared your different points of view and realized the large gap that exists between you.

This is a somewhat pessimistic (though, we feel, realistic) example. It is not a frequent phenomenon, but a case that might well be encountered. It is pessimistic in the sense that no professional help is eventually offered to the teacher, apart from a clarification of the part that values play in education. However, what is likely to happen when you don't realize that there are big differences in value positions? If the counsellor succeeds in maintaining his authoritative power position, we suspect that our chameleon strategy is the only possible one for the teacher. On the other hand, if the counsellor doesn't succeed in this, he will soon realize that his advice, his point of view and his criticism are not affecting the teacher at all.

There is one more pair of concepts that might be adopted from the works of Bateson, Watzlawik *et al.* and which will be familiar enough in the age of the computer. Communication is partly digital, which means that it refers to the relatively precise language of verbal symbols. Communication is also analogue; that is, it encompasses a direct, non-symbolic way of sending messages. Digital communication is precise, making possible a range of logical operations: for instance it permits the use of negations. On the one hand, in analogue communication you may report anger by your body language. You may also report anger in a digital way. Further, you may report that you are *not* angry in the digital mode. But it is this type of negation that possible in the analogue mode.

Analogue communication is, clearly, an important part of total human communication. It is important, therefore, in counselling. However, in counselling we usually rely heavily on digital communication and — we must emphasize this point — we should continue to do so. But what it is important to realize is that the meaning attributed to statements in the digital mode is to a great extent determined by the content of the concomitant analogue communication.

When there is a lack of correspondence between the two modes, we usually use the descriptive term 'double communication'.

Not infrequently there are different messages in the one communication, some digital and some analogue. In the digital mode, there is an official message whereas, in the analogue mode there is conveyed a conflicting message, sometimes about how things really are. When there is correspondence between the messages conveyed in both modes, the chances of effective communication are favourable. When this is not the case, the message conveyed at the analogue level often has the strongest effect and is regarded as representing the truth.

Double communication can easily be identified in many educational situations. A familiar situation in higher education is one where the seminar leader, who starts his session by inviting the students to ask questions or participate in one way or another, behaves in such a way as to make the students realize that he does not really mean what he says. His invitation is a polite gesture and you should not, as a sensible student, respond to it as a genuine offer.

A teacher may tell her pupils that she regards them as responsible persons who are able to make their own decisions relating to certain aspects of daily schoolwork. Yet she interacts with the class in a manner that makes her students fully understand that she does not, in fact, consider them to be at all responsible. A vast number of examples could be given: these, we hope, still serve as illustrations to trigger off similar examples from your own experiences which reveal double communication.

Referring to our previous discussion of role perspective, there is always a danger in a counsellor engaging in what is, in effect, double communication even when he is trying to establish correspondence between the digital and analogue messages. He may have wanted to reconsider his role as a counsellor and may, subsequently, have tried to behave according to the new role pattern. However, it is not easy to change one's own behaviour only on the basis of a decision. It also requires practice. Insecurity in the new role behaviour or customary behaviour left over from the abandoned role may convey an analogue message contrary to what the counsellor really intends.

A counsellor trying to follow the strategy presented in this book, for example, may have some problems with behaving adequately. He may find it difficult in the beginning to show real interest in the teachers' own reflective arguments. There are strong reasons for suspecting that the teachers will not accept the counselling strategy (and the roles ascribed to themselves in it) if they experience this kind of double communication.

So, the counsellor has a problem. Too often he doesn't think of it as a communication problem, but as a result of shortcomings in the strategy he is trying to follow. Meta-communication, again, may be a way to sort this out.

Double communication may present a problem in several phases of the counselling process. Just one more will be given here. Our strategy implies that the counsellor should be careful not to impose his own practical theory on the teachers he is working with. At least, he should make a great effort to minimize the role of his own theory. This is a very difficult task. It is certainly not enough for the counsellor to make his intentions clear in this respect. He also has to *show* it through his behaviour.

When a counsellor comes to realize that the analogue level conveys the information that is really effective, he will see that meta-communication can be applied in order to make the participants aware of the relationship between the digital and the analogue level. We may return to the previous examples:

In establishing a role pattern that is somewhat different from what one of the participants expects, meta-communication is almost mandatory in order to avoid uncertainty, confusion and possibly rejection. In our example, the counsellor was unable to perform his intended role adequately. By applying meta-communication, the counsellor can point out his difficulties and explain his intentional role as well as his actual performance, relating this to his own and the teacher's expectations. Technically, this is not difficult to do: the problems usually lie at the attitudinal level. It requires some boldness and personal confidence to express doubts, shortcomings and uncertainty. On the other hand, it is to be expected that the teacher also experiences some degree of doubts, shortcomings and uncertainty. Resorting to meta-communication may be a way of making a difficult situation easier to deal with for both individuals.

Meta-communication cannot successfully be applied once only and then abandoned. It has to be repeated over and over again, with the invitation (at least) to engage in it coming from the counsellor when he finds it appropriate. Usually, brief periods are recommended. One of the major goals is to establish mutual trust which means that the participants realize that there are no real intended differences between the digital and analogue modes. It also represents a training for the teachers that may stimulate them, in turn, to use meta-communication in their teaching when *they* feel it appropriate.

In our second example, the problem was how the counsellor should accommodate his own practical theory within the counselling process. Ideally, his theory should not have a superior position to that of the teacher. The aim should be to develop the teacher's theory, not to inflict on her the counsellor's. We know that in practice this is nearly impossible. This fact is an important one to ensure that the teachers grasp. Probably the only way to achieve this goal is by means of meta-communication.

Over and over again, the counsellor has to make it clear that his points of view, his advice, what he thinks are important issues, etc., all reflect *his* theory and that he considers it to be a problem that he may be implicitly imposing *his* theory in spite of all his efforts not to do so.

Meta-communication applied this way is a means of achieving the adequate functioning of the process of counselling. However, it is more than that. We would consider it to be a major achievement if teachers were able to apply meta-communication in their own classes and were inclined to do so. We definitely do not consider it to be enough to *teach* about meta-communication for future or practising teachers. It has to be experienced many times to show that it in fact works.

The emphasis we put on meta-communication throughout the counselling process is similar to the idea of having a post-conference analysis suggested by Goldhammer *et al.* (1980). However, we would like to have the evaluation of the supervisor(s) (to put it in the words of Goldhammer *et al.*) performed as an integral part of the ongoing counselling and not postponed to the end of the process. This is not a denial of the idea of having a final conference in which attention is focused explicitly on the counsellor, but it certainly means that we prefer an earlier effort to make such a conference more or less superfluous.

There is always a risk that the content of the meta-communication itself operates at the digital level and that there is an analogue-level necessary underneath, saying: 'Don't trust what is being said. It is not like that, after all.' There are also risks involved that meta-communication sessions can become irrelevant, lengthy and even boring if not properly conducted. The skills required by the counsellor here are acquired mainly by practice and reflection in much the same way as teachers have to learn about the importance and functions of meta-communication, as mentioned above.

It has been stated that meta-communication is a tool in counselling (as it is in teaching) but not only a tool. The importance that is given to meta-communication reflects, in fact, a fundamental aspect of our strategy. It reflects as its central values: commitment and concern for the problems of another person, a belief in human and professional development on the basis of that other person's own values and her ability to develop by her own efforts. A fundamental assumption we make is that of the value of a counsellor's role as helper, not as one with the task of shaping teachers to fit a predetermined model. A core feature of our position is that the counsellor should possess the frankness and willingness to accept views, opinions, and values that are contrary to those held by himself. The weight given to meta-communication reflects the professional standpoint that counselling — as well as teaching — is not a 'technical' profession in which the practitioner possesses a hidden strategy that he keeps to himself. Giving high priority to meta-communication is a corollary of the commitment to a, frank, open and outspoken position which defines the role of the counsellor as often as participant and rarely a spectator. Real involvement on the counsellor's part is the clear consequence, it will readily be seen, of our preferred strategy.

5

Relationships, Themes and Perspectives in Counselling

We have tried previously to be quite explicit about our prime interest in our present writing about counselling: we are searching for *a strategy for counselling*, that is, ways to go about securing the arrangement of productive counselling situations. However, counselling has to be about something. There would be no need for a strategy if it were not for the *content* with which it was to deal. Still, we maintain that our prime focus is the strategy; and that it is with *this* in mind that we continue throughout this chapter to discuss what may be a productive content to deal with in the counselling dialogue.

For a counsellor to decide what elements in teaching plans and practice ought to be selected for discussion is — according to this strategy — partly a question of giving priority to the needs and interests of the teacher concerned. But, as counselling also involves a kind of confrontation, the selection of content for the counselling dialogue is a matter of decision for the counsellor as well. Here, we enter into the area of what is important in teaching, an area where the answers certainly differ among counsellors as well as among teachers. In this discussion we want to be as non-prescriptive as possible and to avoid describing in this chapter *the* way good teaching ought to be — and thereby describing the pre-determined end result that some might think is to be aimed at in counselling. This indeed would be quite contrary to the concepts of the counselling strategy we have presented. On the other hand, we are aware of the impossible task it is to write about counselling without expressing any views about good teaching. We therefore try, throughout this chapter, to indicate *three broad areas or categories of content* which *we* would consider it natural to deal with in counselling, without giving any conclusions on the questions raised. Others, of course, may disagree with us even on this level and may accordingly like to emphasize other aspects. They are certainly most welcome to do so.

Before presenting these three areas, however, we want to make two points clear. To us, it is of the first importance to try to identify *what is significant for the teacher*, both in her planning (what it is that really matters for her to try out, and why) as well as in its implementation (what is in the forefront of her mind when she has finished her teaching). This is for us the natural starting point for any dialogue. It is granted, however, that it is not always easy to identify; but efforts should be made to do so. But, as we have also pointed out, there is a need for the counsellor to contribute to the widening of the scope of the discussion in order to draw into consideration problems, information, relationships, themes and perspectives that are not the teacher's immediate concerns. These contributions should preferably be made in relation to what is central in the mind of the teacher so that they are connected with what matters to her.

The other point concerns *superficiality*. There is always a risk in counselling of becoming superficial in what one is dealing with. A distinction made by some of our students (Michelet *et al.* 1981), has been helpful to us. They distinguish between two forms of superficiality. The first one refers to the immediate appearance of phenomena which are on the *surface of the teaching practice* (the way the teacher speaks, whether the writing on the blackboard was clear enough, whether the pupils look interested etc.). This sidesteps the more fundamental aspects and issues of teaching. The other form of superficiality relates to the *surface of the field of knowledge* relevant to the phenomena selected for discussion. It is not possible, during a brief counselling session, to draw upon all the potentially relevant knowledge within education that might be helpful; consequently, an element of this kind of superficiality is inevitable.

While this last form has thus to be accepted (although much may be done to reduce the undesired effects of it; for instance, by combining counselling with studies connected to the counselling process), the first form of superficiality certainly ought to be avoided. Focusing on such surface traits in teaching will not only take up time in discussing petty and unimportant things, it may also lead to the teacher believing that these really are the important things to deal with. Such concomittant learning would certainly be detrimental to her further development.

We can then return to the suggested three areas of potential content to be dealt with in the counselling dialogue. We have labelled them: *relationships*, *themes* and *perspectives*.

The first one deals with the character and qualities of the *relationship* between the teacher, the pupils and the subject matter of teaching. Counselling ought to inquire into the ideas and realities of these relationships from time to time, as they constitute a basic characteristic of any teaching.

The *themes* on the other hand, are represented by traditional teaching (didactic) categories, which may be helpful in calling upon the teacher's ability to think and act according to what might be termed an internal didactic analysis of the professional process in which she is involved.

The third area — the *perspectives* — represent more fundamental philosophical, social and political ways of analysing the teaching process. They serve the purpose of viewing the daily practice of teaching and education in relation to its societal functions.

This may sound somewhat abstract and theoretical. Let us therefore go through the relationships, themes and perspectives in order to clarify them by means of practical examples.

Relationships

The fundamental educational relationship is the triangular one between *pupil, teacher and content*. The way in which this relationship is considered and realized in practice sets the scene for whatever else will be going on in teaching. For analysis we will break the triangle up into two-sided relationships (simplifying, as we tend to do when the world is too complicated to be immediately mastered!). Let us take first the relationship between *teacher and pupil*, on the one hand, and the *content* on the other. A conception of this relationship as one where the teacher is in possession of the content, and works to transmit it to her pupils, will result in a totally different strategy for teaching from a conception where the pupil is seen as the one working to get a grasp of the content with the teacher regarded as assisting in this process. There are therefore good reasons for bringing up this point for discussion in counselling, as an issue that the teacher will benefit from clarifying for herself.

These are only two of the possible representations of this relationship. A number of others may be considered. Content can be considered — by the teacher, the pupil or both — as something that has to be mastered in order to get good marks; something, that is, which it is the teacher's duty to present although in itself it is hardly worth pursuing. This is an instrumental attitude to the content of education which is still quite prevalent in schools. On the other hand, content may be regarded as intrinsically valuable; or as something worth mastering because of its relevance to life situations, its correspondence with personal interests or simply for the sake of its intellectual challenge. The way the teacher looks upon content in these respects is also food for counselling discourses, particularly when it includes considerations about how and why *pupils* see the same thing. It will open the mind of the teacher to the need for, and the different ways of, justifying the content that pupils are invited to deal with in school; and it will also make her consider what her own justification would be, what the official school version is and which of the justifications is the most honest, most effective or even both.

So far about the relationship teacher/pupil — content. The two-sided relationship between the *teacher and the pupil(s)* might also be considered. The teacher may think about this in terms of

A subject — object dimension

Is the teacher to be the subject in the relationship, with the pupil as an object — *something* that may be disposed of at the teacher's will? Or is the pupil considered as much a subject as the teacher, with the same basic rights (for instance to take part in decisions) and capacities (for instance rationality) as the teacher herself? Or is the pupil considered a subject just in theory, but in practice only as far as it corresponds to the interests of the teacher or the school?

Questions like these may appear provocative as they seem to imply that we are being intentionally sceptical about teachers' motivations. However they are important ones to bring up in an open discussion, as the problems they point to really exist in the practice of schools. We think it is better to foster teachers who, while still treating pupils as objects at times, know and recognize it and even try to do something about it, than to train teachers who are neither able nor willing to see and deal with this deep problem, even though they are fond of making general statements of their good intents. Therefore questions regarding such basic relationships should be brought out with reference to specific things that happen or are planned to take place during the work in school, and not be conducted merely on a general, philosophical level.

A symmetric — asymmetric dimension

This may also be a relevant dimension to the relationship between teacher and pupil. Although close to the one above, it is in principle a separate one. It raises the question of whether the teacher and the pupil are on equal terms in their relationship, with subsidiary questions as to when, under what conditions and why (or why not) this can be said to be the case. Even when teacher and pupils have a subject — subject relationship with each other, this does not automatically mean that the relationship is symmetrical. The teacher may still be in a different position than the pupils because of her knowledge and understanding of the content of teaching; or because of her role, position or responsibility. But this asymmetrical relationship can turn into a different one in some teaching situations, as when it comes to a pure inter-human relationship when the teacher abandons her authoritative position. How is this relationship to be handled? What is the teacher's conception of her various positions on the symmetry — asymmetry dimension? What are the practical consequences of this position of hers? How will it be reflected in daily work in class? Is the teacher actually aware of the rather subtle distinctions between the two dimensions mentioned here? Is it meaningful to her to distinguish between them and do they have relevance to her work?

Themes

The *themes* listed below have to some extent been introduced previously. Accordingly they are only briefly presented here. Those who feel that they are not sufficiently familiar with these didactic categories are referred to general introductions to didactics or methods of teaching. To illustrate ways of drawing the themes into counselling, several questions are formulated under each of the paragraphs below. To simplify the presentation, most of them are formulated in a way that is suitable for the pre-teaching counselling. We trust that you are able to reformulate them — as well as to add others — to make them relevant for use in post-teaching counselling as well.

Purpose and aims

This category and most of the others is directly represented in the model or draft for the writing of process-intentions presented in Chapter 3. It deals with both the intentions of the teacher as far as the results of her efforts are concerned and the reasons why these particular results are sought. Very often we have found it necessary to return in counselling to this category, as questions concerning the aims and purpose of teaching are generally dealt with quite vaguely by teachers who have not been trained to be explicit about them. Consequently, it helps them to become more conscious and clear about their intentions at this point when questions are asked such as:

What is it that you *really* want the pupils to learn, when you plan to teach like this? Do you have, in particular, affective aims in mind for this teaching unit or is it a mastery of skills you are aiming at, as indicated in the process-intentions? What do you mean by 'increased mastery of the language' as an aim for the lesson? Why are the aims listed here important ones to pursue? Do you think that if these aims were to be reached through teaching, they would really contribute towards the wider purpose of this course?

As teaching is basically an intentional activity, it is important in counselling to return repeatedly to the 'point of reference' represented by the purpose, aims and objectives that the teacher has in mind.

Content

This category is closely connected to that which covers our deliberations about aims and objectives, but it has an additional component. It deals with the *substance* of teaching — what it is about — and how this substance is selected and arranged. Too often in teaching the subject matter is accepted as a given thing and taken for granted without much consideration. The contents page of course books and the lists of content in course plans or central curricula are more or less automatically taken as covering the subject-matter that is to be dealt with in teaching. The arrangement or structuring of the content as found in subjects, disciplines, cross-disciplinary units, topics or projects is often made on the basis of tradition rather than by appropriate deliberation on the part of the teachers involved. The content of education which could deal effectively with what really matters for the pupils within and outside school and with their relationship to each other has a certain tendency to yield to the formal, authorized content of books. Accordingly, it is important in counselling to ask questions such as the following: Why have you decided to focus on just this content in your teaching? Do you think this subject matter could be better dealt with if it were integrated with content that is traditionally associated with another discipline? Why have you chosen to organize the content in this logical way, which corresponds to the structure of knowledge in the discipline, instead of in accordance with a 'psychological' structure that would be more natural for the pupil? Do you realise that this particular selection of content, structured in this way, points to a general problem contained in any subject matter you may want to take up in teaching? To what extent and in what way have you planned to involve the pupils themselves in the selection of the content of the course?

Teaching methods and learning arrangements

This is probably the category that is most often in evidence in the teachers' process-intentions, as they will naturally be pre-occupied with *how* to teach. However, we have noticed a tendency for them to express themselves in quite general terms at this point: 'I will use group work', or 'I will make a short presentation myself and then continue with a class discussion'. Teachers often find it difficult to be more specific, giving a description or specification of what these labels mean. You will have noticed that the draft of process-intentions is quite detailed. This is meant as an attempt to lead the teacher beyond the use of 'method labels' to a more thoroughly considered description of certain things: what the pupils will be doing, what kind of experiences they ought to be having what climate or atmosphere should characterize the situation as well as what she herself is supposed to do.

It is probably important for the counsellor to be aware of the danger that many inexperienced teachers, resorting to their own school experience, will use teacher-centred methods characterized by the supposed transmission of knowledge from teacher to pupils, rather than discovery-based and pupil-active methods. Inexperienced teachers as a group rely heavily on these more traditional methods in their teaching due to their strong memories of the style of teaching that was common in their own school-days. The emphasis on a description of what the *pupils* should do — as well as (afterwards) on what they actually did — may therefore help to focus attention on the learner who is at the centre of any educational enterprise.

Questions like these may be relevant: What do you mean by saying that you will use an inductive approach in your teaching? Do you think that you will achieve the aim suggested, of developing the pupils' curiosity about the subject matter, if you teach by means of a one-way teacher presentation of it? Is the task suggested for the problem solving sequence suitable for group work, or is it rather a task that the individuals in the group must deal with on their own? How do you think the pupils will actually *experience* the method you suggest? Why precisely have you decided to teach just this way? Can you think of an alternative that might forward, say, the skill-element in your aims more effectively?

Pupil characteristics

Teaching has to be closely related to the characteristics of the pupils involved, whether this be to their *general* level of development, age or ability, their interests, skills, previous knowledge or their background, habits etc. or *individual* characteristics. Teachers in training are, however, naturally so preoccupied with *their* part in the teaching-learning relationship, that the consideration of such pupil characteristics appears most of the time to be less central to them. This makes it even more important to focus on the pupil characteristics in counselling, both to increase the probability that the teaching will be adjusted to these characteristics and thus be more successful and to draw the teacher's preoccupation away from her own person and interests and towards the pupils'.

Possible questions to ask in this connection may be: Is there any reason to believe that this task is too complex, as it is presented in your plans, to be mastered by pupils of this age? Have you checked whether the pupils are already familiar with the group-work skills required for participating in this activity, or do you need to set aside time in your teaching for them to learn this first? How will you handle the simple problem arising from the different speeds at which pupils in the class are able to work in solving these problems? How are you going to take the reading difficulties of, say, Jim and Mary into consideration in the activity planned for the class? Can this way of solving the problem be justified, having in mind their right to have a learning situation adjusted to their needs and abilities? What about the relation of any such individual work to the rest of the class and their legitimate interests?

Evaluation

Evaluation is a critical factor among our didactic categories. It relates what goes on in teaching, as well as the results of it, to various criteria, in order to make a judgment. It includes both the formal evaluation, which is so often accompanied by marking or grading, and the informal one, whether it is carried out by the teacher or by the pupils. As the aims and purposes of teaching are often involved in evaluation as criteria, reference to these will be relevant, even if this is not necessarily made in the teacher's plans or practice.

As evaluation often functions for the pupils as the manifestation of what *really* counts in school — namely, what is in fact emphasized in evaluative practice — it is also important that teachers too are made aware of the conditioning effect that evaluation has in daily school work.

Questions concerning evaluation may be of the following kinds: Have you consciously planned to include some evaluation in your teaching? Are there any situations in which you can foresee that you will be making evaluative judgements during the lesson? Are you using evaluation to emphasize what is important in the aims of the teaching unit, or is there a discrepancy between your aims and your evaluative criteria? Who is the 'evaluator' in this situation? Very often the teacher is doing the evaluation. Is it possible in any way in this bit of teaching to work towards the aim you have set yourself of making the pupils more critical towards their own work in the subject? Are there any risks of unintended effects in letting the pupils evaluate each other's work in the way you have suggested? How can these be avoided?

Frame factors

As a didactic category, frame (or, if you like, framework) factors are intended to cover the possibilities and limitations given by the resources, premises, rules and regulations surrounding the teaching. It is here used in a rather restricted sense compared to the 'all-inclusive' use of the term for instance, by Lundgren (1972). It relates to the time, equipment, room, material, money, staff assistance etc. provided in a specific situation. It also includes the organisation, decision-hierarchy, rule system etc. which is part of the background against which plans for teaching must be considered. Particularly for teachers in training, who come on teaching practice to a school which they do not know in advance, these matters are often points of information which have to be provided by the counsellor. In this context, the student teacher cannot, of course, be expected to know that in this particular school the head must be consulted for consent if field trips are to be organized or that there is a reservation system for the use of the film-projector. Such particular *information* must, therefore, be provided by the counsellor. The task in *counselling*, on the other hand, is to help draw the attention of the teacher towards a general consideration of the frame factors surrounding *any* teaching.

To do this, questions like the following may be pertinent: Do you think the room available will permit the kind of grouping you have planned? How are you going to arrange the seating to make the arrangement possible? When you plan to concentrate work in the class for a longer than usual period of time on this project, how will you rearrange the normal time-table of the class during this period and how will you deal with the consequent interference with other teachers' work in other subjects? How much time have you planned to set aside for the project? What will you eventually leave out of what was formerly planned in order to make room for the project? What must be done to provide sufficient material if the class starts on a project like this? Does it involve others in such a way that permission must be obtained in advance? Can any of the frame factors contribute to explaining why the last phase of the completed project was too busy and partly unsuccessful? How could this have been handled differently? When more relevant printed material was not available (even though we tried to provide it in advance) how could we have changed the project to make it successful?

Interrelationship between the didactic categories

Above, the different factors mentioned — in the form of didactic categories — have been treated as more or less isolated from each other. This may lead to the incorrect view that such ought also to be the case in counselling. The opposite is, in fact, our intention. Counselling ought to emphasize the *intimate interrelationship between the categories* and the need to consider them not one by one, independently, but as a totality. If the starting point of the discussion is taken from some question of teaching method, this is not best treated as a methodological question only. On the contrary, it may prove more fruitful to relate it to the wider questions of aims, purpose and content. What is it that we try to achieve by using this particular method? Is this in accordance with the aims we have stated for our teaching? Are these aims sufficiently diverse in relation to the more general purpose of the teaching? Would another method provide a better chance of reaching those particular aims? Would another part of the content of the subject be better for illustrating the particular points we want to draw attention to?

In the same way, these considerations may be supplemented by those concerning evaluation or pupil characteristics: If the method is in accordance with the aims, will the evaluation suggested pull in the same direction or does it focus the attention of the pupils on things we do not consider as important as aims? Do all the pupils have the right capabilities for taking part in the activity suggested? How are we going to handle this problem of a mixed-ability range of pupils in relation any particular method we plan to use?

Other themes may also be connected with the one with which we started: Does this method require any particular material or resources that we have to think of and provide in advance? How much time will it take to carry this out? Are we making our plans without sufficient consultation with the pupils, thus putting them in the position of irresponsible objects?

Altogether, in counselling we should try to create the kind of process of reasoning which characterizes the activity of well-qualified teacher in her pre-teaching and post-teaching work. We do not mean to imply that there is unanimity about the characteristics of such work. To us, however, a conscious and critical examination of the different didactic categories and — particularly — the interrelationships between them, as illustrated above, is an important element in such work, and should accordingly be in evidence throughout the counselling discourse. The reservation must again be entered however, that overloading the counselling situation should be avoided, particularly in the initial phase of the relationship. However, it is still possible to draw attention to interrelationships between the categories by bringing more than one of them at a time into consideration.

Care should also be taken to tie the discussion to the real here-and-now-situation, avoiding the type of irresponsible, free-floating discussion that is merely carried on 'in principle'. Teaching takes place in a definite historical and social context which must be taken into account when discussing and deciding what to do.

Perspectives

So far we have been dealing with the *relationships* and the *themes* that may prove central in counselling discussions. Let us also introduce some *perspectives* through which these may be regarded. By this we mean that when teaching is discussed in counselling sessions — before and after teaching has taken place — it may be helpful for the counsellor (as well as for the teacher) to have at his disposal some perspectives which may serve the purpose of directing attention to ways in which the relationships and themes may be analysed. They may provide examples of ways of going *beyond the more restricted analysis* characteristic of themes or diactic categories. Other people have chosen different terms for quite similar phenomena. In Lewis' & Miel's terminology (1972, p. 236), the term 'framework' is used (with reference to Huebner): 'aesthetic', 'ethical' and 'political' frameworks are given as examples. The use of 'each framework', they say, 'would provide a different view of the same whole' — as we would say about the choice of different perspectives. Examples of such perspectives may, however, possibly lead to a better understanding of our position than a further abstract explanation.

Intentions and effects

Teaching is in its nature intentional. We act with purpose in order to fulfil certain intentions. However, we always run the risk of getting different results from those intended. These may be results that replace those we were aiming at as well as additional results. We may safely say that teaching often has unintended outcomes. In many instances this is quite acceptable, as the outcomes achieved may be quite in line with the general goals we have set. And teaching should not (and, indeed, could not) be so one-dimensional and pre-planned that only closely specified results would be regarded as satisfactory. But some outcomes are contradictory to the aims we pursue. (Quite another complication is that the aims themselves may also be mutually contradictory due to an inherent conflict in the ideology of the school). Briefly we may put the label of *intentions and effects* on this perspective on teaching.

Merely stating this fact is, however, not sufficient for those practising within education. It is a problem which needs to be handled daily in educational planning and practice, and which requires open eyes and courage in analysis and evaluation. Quite often we manage happily to ignore the disturbing fact that things turn out to be quite different from what we intended them to be. We manage to overcome this disturbing inconsistency simply by labelling the activities and results in our teaching with terms borrowed from our vocabulary of intentions. We may, for instance, have intended to establish good contact with the pupils during the lesson. We then walk around the class as the pupils are working on their assignments, giving a helping hand, reminding them to concentrate on their work, answering questions etc. Then, more or less regardless of the actual effect this may have had, we are later able to characterize what was going on as 'good contact with the pupils'. To many of those present in the classroom, the activity of the teacher may have been experienced as a controlling and disciplining surveillance; or, equally, as a demonstration of who were seen as the 'good guys' and who were not, judged by the kind of comment made by teacher during her contact-making activity. Although this was not intended by the teacher, it had the effect described, at least for some of the pupils; thus the effect of this particular piece of teaching behaviour is a quite different one to that planned.

A series of other examples may be provided. We want to foster critical thinking in our pupils. We demonstrate for them the way to think critically about a text or a situation; and we end up by having them uncritically accept our criticism! We want to teach the class about the history of our country. We provide them with material that can give exact answers to the detailed questions on the worksheets we have prepared. As a result, they may certainly reach the intended objective of mastery of historical knowledge, but at the same time we have also — unintentionally — taught them that, in history, there are absolutely right answers to be found in books. We have also reinforced their previous learning that, at school, questions are asked by those who already know the answer — particularly of those who can be suspected not to know! (The briefness of the examples must serve as an excuse for a certain simplification made in these statements.)

In our experience the perspective of intention/effect is one which we have found to be valuable. It is also closely connected with the two phases of counselling: before and after teaching. Pre-teaching counselling is by definition limited to a discussion of intentions on a hypothetical level as far as both aims and teaching process are concerned. In the post-teaching session, we have access to empirical 'evidence' as well and may be in a better position for a realistic intention/effect discussion. Still, even in pre-teaching counselling a discussion of potential effects (unintended outcomes) may be relevant: we can try to foresee whether they are *likely* to occur as a result of what we are planning. Of course it is not an aim to avoid completely any unintended consequences. But we must try to anticipate them and decide whether we are willing to accept them, so to speak, as by-products of the teaching process. As mentioned earlier, this perspective is equally relevant for the analysis of *counselling* situations.

Some of the other perspectives mentioned below also have an intention/effects element woven into them, making them sometimes difficult to separate strictly from each other. The important thing about the perspectives, however, is not for them to be mutually exclusive. Rather they should be regarded as somewhat different, although partly overlapping, angles from which the teaching may be viewed. To get a sufficiently multi-faceted picture, it is necessary to use more than one perspective.

Socialization and the culture perspective

The perspective of *socialization* may serve as another example. The way the term is used here is to refer to the process through which a growing person comes to share the wisdom, rules, values, beliefs etc. of the society of which he or she is a member. It must accordingly be regarded as a wider concept than education: including educational processes as well as activity that is initiated by other agents than educators and through other channels, institutions or media than the school.

An example from a quite different field may serve as an illustration. In industry, where careful consideration of safety regulations is a critical factor, courses may be run for the employees to inform about and enforce the existing safety regulations. These courses may be excellent with a good chance of having an effect on the general safety situation in the firm. However, if the course takes place within a general atmosphere of carelessness and a 'who-cares-about-the-regulations' attitude between the persons actually working there, the socializing effect of this attitude may far outweigh the educational effect of the course, the result being no real and lasting influence on the safety within the firm. This result may be difficult to understand with reference to the educational measures alone: one needs also to consider the totality of the socializing forces at work. Similar examples are easy to find regarding education for the development of an ethical code within a profession — wherever there is a significant gap between what is taught and what actually is illustrated in vocational practice. The socializing effect of observed practice will often overrule the ideal communicated through teaching.

The same perspective may give insight in other forms of education; and may serve equally well in counselling. Questions can be asked about the socializing effect of the way the teaching or the school is organized in relation to the *message* transmitted through teaching. The message in a certain lesson may contain strong elements of an ideology where independence and personal responsibility are valued. At the same time, the actual situation in the class and the school may be structured in such a way that dependence is demanded of the pupils and opportunities for giving and taking real responsibility are very few indeed. Another example is when the message of co-operation is presented to the pupils within a framework which favours competition. The socializing effect of the structures or frames within which teaching goes on — 'the hidden curriculum' in Jackson's (1968) term — may be very strong, and this is really worth while drawing attention to in counselling.

Two other examples of it may broaden the scope of this perspective. The first is where there is a contradiction between the message of the school and the prevailing values or practice between the pupils themselves. The school's efforts to teach equality can easily be overridden by the prevailing practice between influential pupils of favouring the strong ones at the expense of the weak and of being extremely inconsiderate to less able individuals.

The second example draws the attention of the teacher to the different 'cultures' or 'sub-cultures' from which her pupils come, and in which they spend a large part of their day; and to the socialization taking place here. The socializing agents in some of these cultures are likely to have quite different values than those of the school, and the effect of these differences in primary socialization on the pupils is important for the teacher to be aware of. The writings of Bernstein (1971) and others working in this field are illustrative of the aspect of socialization mentioned here. (See also Arfwedson, 1979.) The didactic category of 'pupil characteristics' ought also to be considered under this perspective, from time to time in counselling, to broaden the understanding of its consequences for teaching and learning.

Roles

The *role-perspective*, which may serve as a third example, has already been dealt with to broaden the reader's grasp of the counsellor — teacher relationship. It applies equally to other educational relationships, such as that between teacher and pupils. As a part of the counselling procedure, the teacher should from time to time be invited to consider the teaching planned or implemented from this perspective of roles. As the central roles in teaching are complementary, defining one implies, as we have seen, to some extent defining the other. Which role is the teacher defining for her pupils? Are they aware of the behaviour expected of them? Do they accept the role they have been assigned? Do they have the capacities required for carrying out such a role; and are the structural and material conditions around them such that the role may be performed satisfactorily?

An increased awareness of the role-patterns in different forms of teaching may lead the teacher both to an improved understanding of factors at work in her teaching as well as to an acceptance of the consequences of this in further practice; for instance, she may become much more explicit in her communication with pupils about the roles implied in a teaching plan.

Micro — macro perspective

Counselling frequently runs the risk of becoming myopic. The details in the actual classroom situation take on exaggerated dimensions simply because they are so close; and they are even put under a kind of magnifying glass as a result of the vigilant presence of the counsellor. Consequently, it is often difficult to establish that perspective in which the classroom teaching is seen as part of a larger context.

It is, therefore, an important part of the counselling process to help the teacher to establish the habit of perspective-shifting; to vary between the use of a wide-angle and a closer view of her own work. Sometimes we stare so intensely at the problems, the progress, the learning or the failing of a particular pupil in a class, that we forget to see that this is happening as part of a larger picture. Thus it may be the counsellor's task from time to time to ask such questions as: How can the events of the lesson be understood as part of what goes on in the whole school? How can the latter be understood as an example of the school as a social institution? And what broadening of understanding may be achieved by considering the school as, to some extent, a reflection of the society of which it is a part?

In other words, it is a part of counselling to put teaching within the different perspectives of the individual, the class, the particular school, the social institution and the society. Missing out any of these means missing a perspective inherent in teaching as a cultural phenomenon.

The ideological perspective

In this context we use the term 'ideology' in the special sense of 'a limited or false explanation', as it is used in the Marxist tradition. The underlying idea is that some 'explanations' of phenomena or practice are false: a more penetrating scrutiny will reveal quite different explanations as the real ones. These purported explanations hide a reality which it is in someone's interests to withhold from common knowledge.

Many explanations in education have an ideological function. Educational customs are often justified with reference to 'common practice', 'practical arrangements within the school' or 'prescriptions in the curriculum'. And, of course, these can be in many instances quite valid justifications. However, they may also serve as an easy 'excuse' for not considering the educational practice more thoroughly; for not looking behind the immediate reasons for its existence. We can find many different 'explanations', ranging from those of an unreflective tradition with little justification to those that are politically motivated and are not at all in accordance with the officially stated aims of the school. We are not, of course, suggesting that this is due to any malevolent scheme of either the teacher or the school. In most cases it is a relatively unconscious phenomenon, hidden under the routines of the day.

And this is precisely where the counselling comes in. The job of the counsellor, working within this perspective, is to help the teacher to become aware of the ideologies that influence her work and to be reasonably suspicious of the explanations of practice which she herself — as well as other people — is at first inclined to offer. Looking behind immediate explanations will be for her, to some extent, a threatening experience, as she does not know what she may find. Such 'myth-cracking' therefore, is an activity which requires a certain amount of self-confidence on the part of the teacher, as well as confidence in the counsellor. In many cases, it will also require a certain amount of broadly 'political' awareness and understanding.

Other perspectives might have been spelled out. Some of them would be somewhat 'internal' to the teaching situation (like a perspective dealing with the communication pattern in teaching), while others would be of an 'external' (or 'macro') nature (like a perspective dealing with the kind of qualities developed in the pupils through teaching compared to those qualities — both explicit and latent — required by society). Some would be of a sociological nature, others of an economic, ideological or political nature. They must be selected by the counsellor and the teacher; and they will probably vary in accordance with their potential for throwing light upon the specific teaching in question as well as with the values held by the counsellor and the teacher and with the current educational issues in the community around. Our advice to the counsellor is to try not to be held captive by a single or a strictly limited set of perspectives, but to be versatile and to include perspectives which are likely to benefit the individual teacher in a particular counselling situation.

Part of the competence of a counsellor, in fact, has to do with his aptitude for shifting pespectives freely according to what looks promising for the development of the teacher as an independent and reflective professional person.

6

Implementation of the Counselling Strategy

Problems of counselling in general

Throughout this book, it has been a major concern to stimulate persons engaged in counselling with teachers to apply a reflective and deliberate counselling strategy. As regards *our* strategy, we have found it to be to some extent contrary to teachers' initial expectations. They are often more concerned than we are about behavior rather than thought — just to mention one difference. However, any initial discrepancies are normally easily overcome through use of metacommunication, at least in cases where a single counsellor holds the field.

Sometimes, however, teachers become involved with more than one counsellor, as is often the case in teacher training where the student works with several persons guiding him as well as supervisors and assessors from college. A counsellor applying a strategy similar to ours will, it will be realised, have little chance of success unless his colleagues are applying a counselling strategy which reflects the same basic principles. It is obvious that a counselling group must act as a real team; that is, the various members of the group must follow the same strategy. If not, the discrepancy between competing or conflicting strategies of counselling must, at least, be made explicit to the students.

The idea of a coordinated strategy of counselling is often rejected, not because of disagreement with the principle itself, but because it is assumed to be too difficult to reach an agreement on what kind of counselling strategy should be adopted. This problem should not be overlooked. On the other hand, this and related problems in this area are often regarded as more difficult than they in fact are.

It is often argued that an agreement about a counselling strategy implies agreement about teaching in general. If this were the case, it would indeed be a difficult task to agree on a satisfactory measure of counselling practice. However, it is our conviction and experience that an attainable ideal is a situation in which different counsellors *do* comply with the one counselling strategy while holding different views on teaching.

A good opportunity of learning about teaching is when confronted by different views and practices. And — which is more important — it is in this way that the teacher is made familiar with the teaching realities towards which she is supposed to take up her own personal position on the basis of personal value priorities, experiences and theoretical knowledge. A variety in the teaching practices encountered by any teacher is needed. Following this varied experience, the counselling that the teacher is exposed to should encourage reflection upon the alternative she is now becoming familiar with.

Counselling with a student teacher should encourage her to try out unfamiliar teaching methods in order to expand her repertoire. Ideally, the pre-counselling should identify possible teaching methods which the candidate herself would like to try in her teaching practice. There is probably no need for us to make it clear that there are both practical as well as ethical limitations to this general principle. After all, it must be remembered that a student teacher enters a class as a guest and must comply, to a certain degree with the program of the class: she has no right to consider a teaching practice classroom to be her personal experimental laboratory. Obviously, it is the responsibility of the counsellor to see to it that the rights of the pupils as to the sequencing of material and the quality of its teaching are secured. However, a student teacher also has a legitimate right during teaching practice to gain *some* diverse experiences. We suspect that on most teaching practices, the rights of the pupils are given more consideration than the rights of the student teachers. It is no surprise that this often happens, as in this way the counsellor's own way of teaching, which is likely to be pupil-centred, predominates — albeit, without his fully realising it!

A student teacher's right to some experimentation is not exclusive. Among other things, the counsellor is responsible for putting on 'the emergency brake' when needed. The student teacher, being unskilled at the outset, might want to perform her teaching in a way the counsellor cannot accept, as he has to consider the well-being and rights of the pupils. However, when the counsellor finds it necessary to put on the emergency brake, his reasons for doing so must be explained to the teacher in a way that fosters her learning and certainly not in a way that is embarrassing or threatening to her. The way the counsellor handles a situation like this can destroy a teacher's self-confidence and pride in her work; but it also can turn out to be an event from which she learns an important lesson. The problem here is obvious: that it will not be a learning situation for the teacher if it is destructive of her self-confidence. This is something a counsellor himself must learn well!

It is probably not difficult to find examples of counsellors handling the emergency brake problem unsatisfactorily. However, this is fortunately not a frequent problem in counselling. It is far more common for counsellors to apply reinforcement principles that are without doubt theoretically sound and empirically valid but which have questionable relevance to the counselling processes.

A principle in learning psychology which bears on this matter is the superiority of positive reinforcements to negative ones. (The principle may be stated in different terms within various learning theories.) In addition, every counsellor knows that it is a stressful and embarrassing situation to have one's own performance examined. Consequently, counselling is often characterized by a deliberate and strong positive attitude on the part of the theory-influenced counsellor.

The problem here is that — despite the counsellor's wish to counsel in an effective way by the application of relevant learning principles as well as principles from social psychology — the teacher in question may experience the counsellor's behaviour quite differently. It may be conceived as a lack of real interest in the teacher's professional skill and in her problems. The teacher may believe that the counsellor finds her teaching so trivial that he doesn't think it is worth engaging in a dialogue with her about it. If the teacher experiences the counsellor's attitude in this way, what he says will have little significance for her.

The counsellor's positive attitude may even become what can be called a 'humiliating positivism'. The *teacher* may indicate that she was not satisfied with all aspects of her teaching, but her questions and doubts are not really taken seriously. Instead, the counsellor may in fact try to convince her that it was not bad — it was not bad at all; and besides, we all have those problems, particularly in this class etc. The counsellor may thus behave in a way that defines the role of the teacher as an incompetent or even an almost childish person. This indulgent, humiliating positivism may be identified if you compare your attitude when counselling a beginner from a teacher training institution with your attitude when counselling a colleague of yours.

What has been said so far should not lead to the conclusion that the counsellor can afford to be insensitive to the personal need of most teachers to have positive feedback. Of course he should be kind, positive and comforting. At the same time, however, he must be honest with the teacher. He must decide how much frankness and outspokenness she might benefit from — taking into account the various phases of the counselling process.

A counselling session is a co-operative analysis of an educational experience; a mutual sharing of views between a professional and an unskilled person or between two professionals. The actual experience under consideration is, however, a *shared* experience only to a limited extent. There is a difference between the counsellor and the teacher which, it must be insisted, can never be eliminated completely. The counsellor can never obtain the perspective of the true participants in the teaching episode.

In most cases, it is a definite disadvantage for the counsellor to keep a greater distance from the teaching process than is strictly necessary. When possible, it is profitable to join the participants, thereby getting some of the feeling and experiences of the teaching process that they have themselves. It is important to keep in mind, however, that it is impossible for the counsellor to obtain the same experiences as the participants during the teaching unit. The point is that the counsellor should bring himself as close to the participants' situation as possible. At too great a distance, it is simply impossible to get that experiential familiarity which is needed for counselling on an informed basis.

Problems of implementing the proposed strategy

The counselling strategy proposed in this book differs, to a certain extent, from most participants' initial expectations. The most common concerns teachers have are those of getting direct advice or guidance on how to act in specified situations, as well as feedback on their classroom activities. As stated before, our broad aim for counselling is the development of each person's practical theory and, subsequently, a change in teacher behaviour: it is not merely compliance with any advice offered by the counsellor. For teachers to benefit from the strategy, a minimum requirement is familiarity with the intentions and practices of the strategy. However, maximum benefit from it requires rather more than that.

One problem relates to the correspondence between the teaching of educational theory and the application of the counselling strategy. The problem has some resemblance to a Chinese box.

Student teachers attending courses in educational theory are, of course, exposed to teaching; that is, to the same activity that they will later engage in as professionals. Their study program generally consists of three main parts. One is the study of the subjects which they will be teaching. The other is educational theory; and the third is educational practice. The following discussion will relate mainly to the second and third parts.

During their study of educational theory, student teachers not only learn the content prescribed in the syllabus but they also learn something from the way their tutors teach that content. They learn, that is, from the way their professors act as teachers. In previous sections we have discussed the problem of double communication. There might be an hidden message implicit in the teaching of educational theory just as there is in counselling, as we saw. The message might be that educational theory is one thing and what we do when practising is another. There might, in fact, be the message that theory is something 'bookish' which is almost impossible to apply in practice or even unimportant or irrelevant to the practice of teaching. We would, of course, like to think that educational theory is not like that; and we assume that teacher training tutors hold the same view. The point is that the study of theory should deal with content that is relevant to practical teaching and that its presentation ought to make this relevance visible.

The teaching which the student teachers receive in college may be regarded in the same way as are teaching units in the counselling process. The college tutor also has process-intentions for his teaching. These, however, usually remain unknown to his students. We believe that at least some of the lessons in educational theory should be subjected to the same kind of explicit presentation and analysis as is required of student teachers in their practice. In this way, the students may be led to understand the values and functions of process-intentions before they even start their teaching practice and also to realize the relevance of educational theory. The tutor's process-intentions should not, however, be just a demonstration of his skill in writing a document of this kind, but be an honest invitation to a dialogue about the teaching processes he is sharing with his students.

Preparing the student teachers for teaching practice should not be the sole responsibility of the counsellors who work in the schools where the practice takes place. It is quite rightly the responsibility of the college tutor as well, as is the normal practice in Britain. And it is quite reasonable to expect him to make the students competent in planning their teaching — not only on a purely theoretical level but also at the level of practical detail. The difficulty is that real planning requires knowledge about situational factors; and when no real situation is at hand, there exists little possibility for real planning. But, in this respect, it must be pointed out that teachers and students have teaching sessions together in college all the time. It is *these* that can serve as shared examples of real teaching.

So, every possibility to make student teachers familiar with those elements that are applied during counselling ought to be exploited while they are being taught. The utmost care should be taken to avoid double communication within the teaching of educational theory; this suggests a separation between those teaching theory and those counselling on teaching practice, as well as with those involved in the professional counselling process. Admittedly, this is a complex and difficult task.

There is a *second problem* involved in applying our strategy in some fields. We rely heavily on process-intentions for teaching units. What, then, if a teacher is unable to prepare a counselling document for units she is going to teach?

A retired seaman is engaged to run courses within adult education in a coastal area. He has no formal educational background for this and has never taught before. He considers his task to be that of performing the work operations his students are to learn and not that of actually teaching the skills. When asked to explain how he wants to arrange the teaching of his course, or even one specific session within it, he may not be able to do so. At least, what he gives to you is not a statement of any value to the counselling you want to undertake with him.

In adult education (and some other cases in which the teacher has no formal training for teaching) this is a big problem. Does it mean that our strategy is inappropriate in such situations?

It should be noted that an inability to prepare a counselling document does not mean that some practising teachers have no practical theory governing their teacher behavior. It is our conviction — and one of our basic assumptions — that everyone who is teaching possesses a practical theory, even though they may not be aware of its existence. The theory may not contain much relevant, conscious knowledge. It may be totally unreflective. But it is there!

An apparent lack of practical theory and a consequent inability to prepare a counselling document has to be taken into consideration in the counselling process. In particular the pre-teaching counselling has to be modified so that more help is given to the teacher in making her intentions explicit. Care has to be taken, of course, to identify the teacher's real concerns and to let them have the greatest influence on the process-intentions.

A woman is running some classes in adult education, teaching the national traditional oil painting. She has herself been trained mainly by local craftsmen. She is now working on her own and has been engaged to teach painting to people in her neighbourhood who want to learn the skill for leisure activities.

She participates in a course on 'Practical teaching skills', together with others who teach either theoretical subjects or practical activities in adult education in the same district. Much of the course consists of teaching units performed by the participants with the others acting as students. Our teacher is reluctant to perform in this way, expressing doubts about her own teaching skills. She doesn't know how to teach. It is teachers in theoretical subjects who do that sort of thing. The teaching is to be video-taped as well!

Later in the course she decides to have a go anyway. Her counselling document is very brief indeed, consisting of a bare schedule for the lesson, a mixture of objectives (show some techniques with a brush, teach how to preserve brushes etc.), a few activities (I will paint a rose) and so on. During pre-teaching counselling, it is not possible to make her elaborate on her counselling document. She is upset and anxious, and this is projected into evident worries about whether the equipment she will be needing will be present or not.

During the post-teaching session, she is totally negative about her own performance and states repeatedly that she wants to have a clear-cut, condensed recipe for success. We are all eager to give her positive feedback, but she doesn't regard us as being honest with her.

Then, we play back a part of the recorded teaching session. She is very upset about the way she looks on the screen. However, we have all been involved as participants in her lesson and appear on the recording as definitely eager to learn. She does not notice this behaviour of ours during the lesson until we ask her to look at it instead of concentrating on herself only.

When she realizes the interplay between herself and the other students and notices our positive involvement, she broadens her perspective. At this stage she has sensibly realized that she can expect no easy recipes from us, so she starts reflecting herself. She recognizes the need to have her instruction built up progressively, identifying each separate part of the skill and stressing the cumulative nature of the separate parts. The rest of the post-teaching counselling consists mainly of her own evaluation, with the rest of us giving our impressions, experiences, advice and so on.

Now, the main point is that the counsellor in this situation is subjected to a substantial pressure to act as an expert on teaching. In the short term, it would have been very much welcome if the counsellor had started to expose *his* practical theory, applied to her situation. However, in the long term, the effect would almost certainly have been an intensification of her feelings of inferiority and a decline in her reflection and self-confidence. She might have concluded that everyone else always knows what to do and that she herself should quit teaching and continue with her other work.

Teachers with limited educational knowledge usually have a very limited repertoire of teaching methods. More direct advice about different ways of doing it may be needed; and more emotional support may be rquired in order to encourage the teachers to try unfamiliar methods. We don't think, however, that other parts of the counselling strategy have to be changed to any substantial degree; and certainly not its basic principles presented earlier.

A *third problem* also relates to the weight assigned to counselling documents. Not all educational situations can be broken down into discrete teaching units in a sensible way. As an example, this is the case to a greater extent in pre-school and infant teacher training than in the training of the teacher of other age-ranges.

In most cases, a teaching unit is an integral part of a sequenced teaching scheme. It might be a randomly selected part, but it is usually desirable to pick out one that, for some reason or another, is considered to be a promising example of a type of teaching — as judged by the counsellor or, even better, by the teacher.

In the nursery or infant school, it is more difficult to identify a clear-cut educational sequence from which to pick a useful example. And it seems definitely not to be a sufficiently good idea to pick, say, one hour, an afternoon or a day as a teaching unit.

Rather it might be more feasible to identify some different recurring routines in the day (like arrivals, whole-group indoor activities, free play etc.) or some critical incidents that may take place at irregular intervals (like conflicts between children, aggressive play, withdrawing children etc.). Such incidents may also be discussed in anticipation by the counsellor and the student teacher, preferably on the basis of some sort of 'counselling document'; although this will need to be edited a bit differently from the customary document, for obvious reasons.

If the critical incidents have been carefully predicted they will occur sooner or later in the presence of the student, who will then try to act as best she can. At a convenient time later on, 'post-teaching' counselling can then take place with reference to the handling of the incidents and to the precedent counselling.

Notice that teachers have some freedom within our strategy to select teaching tasks that, for some reason or another, are of special interest to them. The same holds for the pre-school 'teaching units'. It is therefore not necessarily the best thing for the counsellor alone to pick out the critical incidents. It is usually better to make it a part of the student's job to identify and prepare for those incidents that she reckons are critical both as to their nature and their frequency.

Contrary to common practice, post-teaching counselling is not always the most important step in the counselling process. In some cases it might even be omitted. The same does not, however, hold for the pre-teaching step. Pre-teaching counselling should in principle never be omitted. It is of great value and the quality of post-teaching counselling depends to a large extent upon the success of it.

It can be added that it is possible to perform post-teaching counselling even in cases where the counsellor cannot be present at the teaching session. It is not an ideal situation, of course, severely limiting as it does the possibilities for effective feedback, but it might be appropriate when it is the only possible way.

A *fourth problem*, related to the implementation of our strategy, has also to do with pre-teaching counselling. In spite of the counsellor's intention to have a teacher make her practical theory explicit, pre-teaching counselling might turn out to become a game of some sort. It might become 'hide and seek', in which the teacher is trying to produce quick and intelligent reasons for her plans, not because she thinks they are important but because they might satisfy the counsellor and make him stop his questioning. The counsellor must understand the teacher's need to present acceptable justifications for her plans and the fact that teachers normally do not consider their reasons and justifications to be sufficiently elegant, advanced or academically definisible.

A difficult and important task for the counsellor is, therefore, to assist the teacher in identifying her real reasons and justifications during the pre-teaching sessions. This is not achieved if the counsellor doesn't have an accepting attitude towards trivial justifications, and it is rarely achieved without distributed bits of meta-communication throughout. The problem usually diminishes gradually, partly as a result of the counsellor's attitude but also as a result of the teacher's increasing awareness of her own practical theory.

This point has some relevance to the post-teaching counselling as well. The counselling document that has been worked out should have a central position in the discussion that follows the teaching unit, however limited their content may be. This is not always the case. When this documentation is not extensive and to the point, it may in fact be rather difficult to pay the required attention to it. In such cases, what usually happens is that the discussion becomes 'evasive'. It has not been precisely stated what the teacher's intentions originally were. So, the teacher — consciously as well as unconsciously — adapts her intentions to what actually happened. The main problem involved is not that the discussion becomes difficult to conduct, but that the counselling becomes less effective. It becomes impossible to identify any correspondence or discrepancies between intentions and realities, and consequently there is less to reflect on; so, there is limited feedback of the kind that eventually could have developed the teacher's practical theory a little further.

The *last problem* we want to look at, briefly, deals with the climate of the counselling dialogue. In our process-intentions for counselling, it is referred to as a process of mutual understanding, wondering and reflection in which the teacher will feel free to explore and develop her own practical theory. This may sound idealistic and far from the reality known to many counsellors and teachers. Some will say that the strategy suggested is one demanding too strong a feeling of security from both teachers and counsellors to have any real chance of successful implementation in practice.

We agree that it is a security-demanding strategy — one that cannot be put into practice overnight. However, our experience is that, given the time to work out and establish new role relationships for the participants in the process, and given the time to communicate during counselling on a meta-level, the counsellor using this strategy has a reasonable chance of success. In working in this way, a certain amount of courage is demanded at the beginning by the counsellor to play the role of the interested helper who will not always know what is right, instead of being the expert. This courage has to be combined with an openness and a willingness to respect other solutions than the one favoured by the counsellor himself. And even granted that there is a great demand on the teacher to be bold enough to enter into a counselling relationship like this, the stronger demand, in our view, is on the counsellor to set the stage for a process that has these characteristics.

Problems of this kind have to be balanced against the possible benefits of using the strategy; and probably also against the problems and results of alternative counselling strategies.

Problems related to various fields of application

Our counselling strategy is intended to be applicable to four main areas. There are specific problems of implementation within each of these. Although there are some problems that might be encountered in several areas, we would like to discuss separately some of the major problems that are likely to be encountered in each of the areas that follow.

We consider, then, the strategy to be relevant in *teacher training*, in any *consultancy service* for teachers in general, in various forms of *course settings* (particularly in courses on teaching skills) and in situations where *teachers (or student teachers) are counselling each other*.

Most of the areas of application are real-life situations: only one consists of an artificial teaching situation. In some there are professional counsellors present and in one of them there is no such person. The course setting may be *part* of teacher training, consultancy services or mutual counselling among teaching colleagues, or it may be independent of these. Because of practical limitations, courses may have to be based entirely on aritifical teaching units or, on occasion, they may be combined with realistic teaching. In order to make the presentation clearcut, we restrict the discussion of course settings to artificial teaching units only.

Application to teacher training

We are not so familiar with teacher training institutions that we feel competent to identify all the specific problems that may occur when the strategy is to be adopted. Besides, teacher training institutions are not all identical.

One set of problems has to do with organizational factors. We have stated in Chapter 1 that our book is a micro-level study of the counselling process considered as a general phenomenon. Our intention is not to point out different counselling strategies that might be appropriate within specific organizational contexts. We are dealing with the principles of counselling with teachers and we leave most of the implementation problems to those who know the organizational context far better than we do.

Traditionally, counselling during teaching practice has been carried out mainly through post-teaching sessions. Student teachers do their teaching practice in institutions with time schedules which leave limited possibilities for pre-teaching sessions. This fact may not be considered to be a significant one. However, an organizational pattern that does not give much opportunity for pre-teaching counselling produces inadequate counselling. Counselling under these circumstances is bound to violate some basic principles with a considerable shift from depth to superficiality.

It is sometimes objected to our strategy that it requires the training of all the school-based counsellors from a large area who are engaged on a part-time basis. We consider this objection to point to a difficulty for all counselling strategies, including ours. If a teacher training institution considers that all its counsellors are performing the counselling of student teachers satisfactorily, then there is no need to adopt a new counselling strategy and to make it known to all involved. If, on the other hand, the institution decides to improve the quality of counselling, the results is a general problem of training the counsellors, whatever strategy is adopted.

As regards our strategy, there is one possibility that should not be overlooked. We have earlier stated our belief that the strategy might offer students more adequate counselling. Our conviction may, of course, be wrong. If it is not, however, it is more or less mandatory that the student teachers are taught about the strategy and stimulated to implement it in their teaching practice periods. This training has to be done as part at the teaching of educational theory in the teacher training institution.

In addition to our disregard of specific contextual factors throughout this book, we have also left out the problem of the relationship between counselling with student teachers and the necessary evaluation of their teaching competence. However, the reader will know that this represents a major problem.

People with a responsibility for the certification of potential teachers might object to the strategy presented. Obviously, there are some students who want to enter the teaching profession who will not have the personal or professional qualities needed to reach an acceptable standard of teaching skill, no matter what kind of study program they receive. Controlling evaluation of students on teaching practice is therefore necessary to secure competent teachers. How is it then within the counselling strategy presented possible to assess in these terms the practical theory of a student teacher, as well as her ability to transform it into practice.

Admittedly, the strategy we propose does not primarily focus on assessment. It has its historical roots in counselling with practising teachers, where problems related to certification do not, of course, exist. Its primary objective is to *improve* a students practical teaching. A college tutor involved in the certification of teachers needs to have criteria of teaching competence which are as objective as possible so that the certification is fair. The problem here is that when counselling is made secondary to certification and the counselling process is adapted to the needs of this certification, it results in a poorer than otherwise quality of counselling; just as the problems related to certification increase when the major concern is with the quality of counselling.

Our own view is that it is extremely difficult to combine a concern for counselling with a concern for proper certification. Rather, one has to decide which concern is most important and then adopt the strategy which is appropriate.

This is less than the whole story, however. It *is*, we believe, quite possible to adopt our strategy without abandoning certification. The criteria applied in assessment must, however, be in harmony with the principles of counselling. It is detrimental to counselling if students are subjected to evaluation criteria consisting of pre-existing standards for teacher competence, regardless of any underlying reasoning and level of consciousness and reflection on the part of those students. On the other hand, if criteria that are intended to assess the consistency, richness, relevance, individuality and integrity of the candidate's practical theory are applied — as we think they should be — the incompatibility between assessment and counselling might well be reduced.

The core of the certification problem is not totally different to that of counselling. In both cases, there is a limited degree of freedom allowed to the student teacher as to the practical theory with which she may operate and, therefore, the consequences of it. When the assessors decide on certification and when we, as counsellors, respond to our student teachers, there will be cases when we all have to conclude that the student's performance is not up to generally accepted standards. The, problem however, is undeniably more pronounced in certification.

There is a strong demand on us to mark out and justify the limits of acceptable practical theories and acceptable educational practice. It is not enough to justify our decisions in these matters with reference only to our own practical theories. This is a fundamental problem in teacher training which we certainly don't aspire to answer in writing about counselling. What should be pointed out, however, is that the always strong demand to have explicit and objective criteria for acceptable teaching practice may lead to a narrow definition of teaching that gives undue predominance to technical skills.

Put another way this means that it is probably easy to judge whether a teacher's practical theory is adequate as regards experience and knowledge. But the real problem may rest in the value aspect of teaching. Which values do we regard as 'adequate' or 'acceptable'? Which are not?

Another problem concerns the mental health of student teachers (and of teachers in general). We think that the presence of some personal problems should not automatically lead to the conclusion that the student or teacher is unfit for the profession. But when personal problems prevent a student from benefiting from a teaching training program — counselling included — we would prefer the student to realize on her own that the teaching profession is not appropriate for her. When this does not happen, the certification problem still, of course, remains.

The tendency in teacher training — in Britain as in the Scandinavian countries — has been towards a pass/fail system of certification as a replacement for complicated systems of differentiated grading. In relation to counselling we regard this as a productive step, which helps to reduce the constraining influence of certification on the process of teaching and on counselling within teacher training. Nevertheless, the above problem still exists!

From our point of view, writing about counselling, we would like to add one warning. During the last few years, students within various parts of the educational system have secured the right to complain about assessment decisions. This is a right which it is vitally important to maintain. So, as to the assessment of practical teaching, the rights of the student may force teacher training institutions to prepare objective criteria, not because criteria of this sort are considered to reflect the fundamental qualities required by teachers, but simply because the document is needed for the complaints procedure. Such criteria can easily destroy any possibility of productive counselling and increase the tendency of students to regard the 'chameleon strategy' as the most effective one to follow.

It might also be argued that this strategy is one that requires more resources than others. If this were true, such an argument might lead to a rejection of our scheme. It is therefore worth searching for measures that make it possible to adopt the strategy without having to expand the costs. One measure we would suggest is to apply group counselling. There may, of course be other justifications for group counselling.

One of the principles discussed earlier pointed to the fact that an important concern, when deciding upon a counselling strategy, is to make the teachers independent of the counsellor. Early in a counselling sequence, it is certainly necessary to have a full-time counsellor involved. Later on, some of the responsibility for providing feedback can be given to fellow student teachers. Probably it would be best for this to happen gradually; and the students should know about it in good time and understand the justification for such an arrangement. In fact, there are several reasons why it may be a sensible thing to do.

One reason is the need to train teachers to work together with colleagues in the practical situation from the start of their careers. Obviously, co-operation among teacher colleagues cannot be expected to happen easily by itself. Too often, teachers hold an attitude towards close co-operation with colleagues that is of the 'my-classroom-is-my-castle' sort. At the very least, we think it is important in teacher training to have the students experience the value of mutual counselling at their own level; and, which is the usual result, to experience the resulting good feeling of mutual concern that comes with the sharing of problems.

There is what we can call a strategic argument as well. Our experience teaches us that feedback coming from a fellow student or a collegue is often more effective than feedback coming from a professional counsellor. At least it is more often given in the kind of language used by the teacher herself. There are, though, some necessary conditions as to the climate of the group that have to be satisfied in order to ensure that mutual counselling within the group runs satisfactorily. The responsibility as to group climate has to remain largely that of the counsellor. And it will normally imply that a group should start with a given counsellor and then continue on their own (with the same members), with the counsellor attending the group from time to time.

Our experience has been that teachers, contrary to their own expectations, have found that there is a lot to learn from group counselling with fellow teachers. It is not only the person being counselled at any one time who is learning from it. The other members of the group usually report on the usefulness of attending such counselling groups. It is also beneficial for everyone participating that there are obligations resting on them all to have a counselling function towards the teacher who is to perform or has already performed a teaching unit. The professional counsellor's task is to involve all the students in the counselling process and certainly not to hold the floor himself.

Consultancy services for teachers in general

The counselling performed in any kind of consultancy service — say, in a teachers' centre — may take a number of forms; counselling with groups or individual teachers, offering courses or individual consultancy facilities, providing materials for teachers, spreading information to teachers and so forth. Given the diversity of activities carried on in any centre, as well as the wide variation in organizational structure to be found, it is not really possible to discuss the general relevance of our counselling strategy in this area.

Fortunately, it can be said that where consultancy centres aim at assisting teachers in the development of their practice, much of our strategy is as valid in this field of application as it is in teacher training. Some important differences exist of course. The point is that a counselling strategy applicable to teacher training should be appropriate for practising teachers as well, in spite of differences in the two. As mentioned earlier, our strategy had its origins in in-service counselling with university teachers and is consequently even more adaptable to the needs of practising teachers than to those of students. We regard this flexibility as a strong point of our strategy (modestly, we hope!)

Application in courses

The courses in which our strategy might be applied could be either a part of teacher training or a part of a consultancy service. We present courses here as a special application of the strategy because of the specifics of implementation they represent. A lot of our own experience is from course situations and we believe that it will be of some interest to present one way of using the strategy in course settings.

In courses, it is often necessary to remove teachers from their daily teaching and use 'artificial' teaching units to represent the real ones. This means that the course participants will have to act as students/pupils. Course settings, therefore, have certain limitations compared with natural teaching sessions.

This artificiality means that the participants on a course miss certain qualities of real teaching situations. At first this may seem to be an unfavourable situation — one which has to suffice when it is impossible to have the best. This is certainly how many participants react before the course has started. The artificiality also means that the transfer of what the participants have learnt to their own teaching situations is made their own individual problem — and therefore rather difficult.

On the other hand, there are also certain advantages to the artificial situation.

Among other things, each participant is placed in the student role, which may be a very thought-provoking and useful experience. Particularly when some time has elapsed since the participants were students, this experience may bring back memories of how it felt to be subjected to teaching.

If we refer to our previous description of process-intentions we see that some of them can only be commented on by the pupils they are aimed at. In a real situation, it is normally not very easy to obtain these comments. Instead, the teacher and the counsellor have often to assume what the participants experienced. In this respect, the artificial situation is superior to the real one, as the participants here can more easily report on their experiences as 'pupils'. Whether these experiences are 'genuine' or not will naturally have much to do with the discrepancies (in age, knowledge and background) between the participants and those whose roles they are playing.

The artificial situation also makes it possible to choose content and methods as one likes; there is no need to take all the frame factors into consideration, as is usually the case. It offers a freedom from the restrictions we usually have to consider. However, there is also the possibility of assuming that the normal restrictions and frames *do* hold in the course situation, thereby making the teaching unit a more realistic one. It can be left to the participants to choose between realism and freedom; realism means more direct relevance to daily teaching but not the same possibility of experimenting, whereas freedom means opportunity to experiment outside the more familiar situations and methods.

We use to encourage teachers to pick a teaching unit that might be of special interest to them for various reasons. This relates not so much to the topic as to the teaching methods. In this approach, certain methods which they may have wanted to try (perhaps without doing so), other methods which they have in fact tried unsuccessfully, or teaching problems which are frequent in their day-to-day teaching, are all encouraged. Any concern about how interesting the topic might be to the rest of the participants is rejected. Apart from this, teachers are free to make their own choices and, above all, to choose a teaching task that is difficult or easy according to the teachers' own judgment. However, we do try to stimulate them to choose a unit that is somewhat risky and certainly not one that is unchallenging and 'safe'.

The choice of a topic for teaching is a major difficulty, at least when university teachers are concerned. It cannot require much knowledge of the subject from the other participants. This imposes severe limitations as to choice of subject matter and relevant topics. In some cases, the teaching may become trivial as the teaching units, restricted in this way, cannot reflect more than some specially limited cases within the subject area.

It might be of some interest to know the practical arrangements of our courses, not because they are planned in a perfect way but in order to explain more fully the application of our strategy to course settings.

Introduction: Three introductory sessions (three hours each). The first two give necessary information about the course, about the strategy (process-intentions etc.) and offer training in the handling of the television equipment (in case the teaching is video-taped). The third session — run in smaller groups conists of pre-teaching counselling

	sessions based on written counselling documents prepared by each participant.
Main part:	The residential part consists of successive teaching units with a video recording of each unit. Counselling takes place on the basis of (revised) counselling documents immediately after each teaching unit, with video playback. All participants act as students as well as acting as counsellors, with the main responsibility for counselling resting with the course leader. A minimum of two hours ought to be allocated to each teaching unit, including the counselling session.
Application part:	Three sessions (three hours each), with a program that is decided in collaboration with the participants. The idea is to try to remedy some of the weaknesses arising from the artificial nature of the main part; for instance, by recording and discussing real teaching situations involving the participants as teachers.

The ideal number of participants is between sixteen and twenty. Two course leaders are needed. The participants are grouped as shown below (for sixteen participants);

I		II
1 2	A	9 10
3 4	B	11 12
5 6	C	13 14
7 8	D	15 16

Each of the four groups (A–D), consisting of four participants each, go through pre-teaching counselling sessions together, with one of the course leaders present as counsellor. Sessions for each group take about three hours. The teachers arrive at the pre-teaching counselling bringing sufficient copies of their counselling documents. These are read by the counsellor and the other participants in the group and discussed one by one. Afterwards, each teacher is free to revise her document in accordance with the comments she has received from the counsellor and the other teachers.

In the main part of the course, there are mainly 'half plenary sessions' with one course leader in each group (groups I and II). As you can see from the figure above these groups are put together in such a way that there is only one person in each group who is familiar with the pre-teaching discussion of the counselling document of any other teacher. This person handles the camera. This arrangement is necessary in order to keep each teacher's intentions unknown to those participating in her teaching unit: the intentions are not made public, of course, until the teaching has taken place.

In addition to the half plenary sessions, there are short plenary sessions every day (for all, of course) in order to share experiences and 'keep the course together'. A course with sixteen participants will have to last three days to enable all participants to teach and go through the post-teaching counselling arranged in this way.

Teachers Counselling Each Other

On the basis of some personal experience of this kind of activity, we believe that the strategy may be found applicable when teachers want to establish professional groups in order to promote the development of their teaching proficiency. We suspect that many teachers would like to help colleagues who want feedback on their teaching, but that they are often reluctant to try because they don't really know how to do it and because they think it is too difficult.

There is an important reason for mentioning mutual counselling among teachers as a separate field of application, in spite of the fact that it does not occur in any systematically organized way. We honestly believe that counselling with teachers is not a job for professional counsellors only. It would be far better if counselling was done *among* teachers and not only *with* teachers. Counselling should not be regarded as the responsibility only of specialists, but as an integral part of normal teacher team-work. Why teachers are so reluctant to engage in this activity is, we admit, a difficult question to answer briefly.

Sarason (1971) and Lortie (1975) present an interesting explanation which connects the lack of any developed collective professional teaching theory for the whole of the teaching force to frame factors and certain privileges connected with the profession. These, according to his view, counteract any development of the necessary conditions for the creation of such a theory.

Application in other training programmes

It is tempting to point to some aspects of the counselling strategy which can be of relevance to other professions than teaching, as ideas for further developments rather than as final solutions.

From our observations, it seems to be the rule that counselling is normally scheduled to take place *after* an activity has taken place and only in rare cases *before*, at the stage of planning, as in the example below.

> The work of a nurse contains a variety of highly challenging situations, both profession-ally and personally. One student was, during her practice period, responsible for one ward in the night. In this ward there was a critically sick, old patient and the student had to sit by the bed while the patient was dying. The next day she met for the weekly counselling session and discussed with her supervisor what she had experienced and how she had responded to the situation as an inexperienced nurse. They had a lot to talk about.

Certainly they had! However, this kind of critical professional challenge should definitely have been analyzed at an earlier stage and the student should have been prepared for it before she was thrown into it. But how?

There is no lack of theory applicable to this situation and the teachers and supervisors have all relevant experience which can be shared with the students. In *addition*, each and every student must be encouraged, or even requested, to do such analyses herself, from her own personal point of view; to anticipate her own emotional reactions and then have access to experienced staff to counsel her on the way she is thinking about it. It is hardly debatable that such pre-counselling can prepare students better.

It is not only in the training of nurses that challenging work situations can be anticipated and prepared for. The selection of 'critical incidents' should observe at least the following criteria:

— Experienced staff with inside knowledge of the work must take part. However, it is contrary to our experience that insiders always manage to do it alone; in many cases it is advisable to recruit an outsider to join in, preferably one who is familiar with training.
— The incidents should be critical, demanding, challenging — not only from a strictly professional, but also from a human, point of view.
— The incidents should be of a kind which make it possible, and quite natural, to look upon it from a theoretical angle. The richer the incident, as to potential theoretical dimensions, the better.
— Although it is not essential that all incidents be so frequent that they are likely to happen during the period of training, it is recommended that at least some do. The occurrence helps the counselling gain in realism and gives opportunities for post-counselling.
— The incidents should be realistic (meaning with relatively normal constraints on action). The student should appreciate that it is worthwhile to work on an abstracted incident, both because of the nature of it and because it is highly likely that when it is encountered, action will have to be urgent and deliberate.

Some examples are offered:

— In the training of general practitioners in medicine: Into your office comes a new, female patient. During your conversation it occurs to you that problems related to alcoholism may be involved. What will you do about it?
— In the training of specialists who prepare for work abroad in a developing country: You receive information, off the record, that there seems to be some justification to suspect one of the senior, local staff of embezzlement. What will you do?
— In training control room operators for offshore production platforms:
The pressure in one settling tank increases over the acceptable limit. On the basis of the documentation provided, what is likely happening? What do you do?
— In management training:
You have to present to the Board a Memo containing suggestions that you antici-pate the majority of the Board members will not favour (more details can be given). How are you going to prepare for the meeting? How will you present your proposal?
— In the training of police officers:
Together with one colleague you encounter a street riot. The radio set proves not to be working. How would you interpret and apply standing orders and regulations in such a case?
— In the training of social workers:
A client in your office is first crying and then suddenly points a knife at you. You cannot get to your phone and you cannot shout for help. What do you do?

These examples are not worked out together with experienced staff and are sug-gested here only as illustrations. Cases like them can be introduced and worked through in counselling sessions in about the same way as in the counselling documents previously described. In some cases, a more comprehensive description is required and, in other cases, counselling sessions can be added to other teaching sessions such as lectures, group work, role plays and simulations in order to penetrate the topics more effectively.

Even in technical training, where it is often considered inappropriate to *discuss* exact phenomena (which, of course, is seldom valid), counselling on the basis of student accounts of planned actions can give superior training in the application of theory compared to other teaching methods. That is, if the expert supervisor is able to refrain from explaining ('It takes so much time to pull it out from the student.') and adopts the role of a counsellor and not the more familiar one of lecturer.

7

Summary of the Main Points

In this book we have tried to outline a theoretical basis, as well as a practical strategy, for counselling with teachers. We do not think, however, that the content of the book is likely to be completely unfamiliar to those involved in counselling. They will usually have rich experience in this field and we are not in a position to compete when it comes to length of experience. However, as mentioned earlier, sound practice cannot be judged on the basis of its length only. So, we have aspired to make a sketch of a *systematic and reflective approach* that is based on the experience of professional counsellors but which also includes an 'outside' perspective.

We have tried to show the importance of a deliberate and well-grounded strategy; that is, a coherent, overall method of going about counselling. We have not given much advice on how to act in specific situations, as we have judged 'tactical' advice of this kind to be inferior to a general strategy.

> The job of a theory is to evoke judgment rather than rote obedience. The application of theory is the bringing to bear of critical intelligence upon practical tasks rather than the implementation of good advice.
>
> (Entwistle, 1971 pp. 101–102).

Most of our arguments have been on an *intentional level*. As we all know, good intentions do not in themselves produce satisfactory educational practice. We need to know how our intentions actually function in practice. As regards counselling, *our* intentions as presented in this book can be summarized like this:

Counselling ought to develop teachers'

— practical theory;
— tendency to act deliberately according to their own theory;
— tendency to develop their own theory through experience and reflective thinking about the experience; and
— independence and the tendency to deliberately change their own educational practice.

These are the main guidelines that have been focused upon.

On the other hand, good intentions are necessary but not sufficient conditions for satisfactory practice, counselling practice included. We need to look at how our practice really operates in order to modify it. According to our view, counselling is inadequate when it reinforces teachers'

— adaptation to the varied philosophies and practices of different counsellors;
— dependence;
— lack of confidence in their own ability and their disinclination to justify and question their own educational philosophy and practice;

— tendency to an uncritical adoption of certain methods, with limited understanding and justification for doing so; and
— tendency to continue existing educational practice unreflectingly.

We are not completely free to create our own work, either as teachers or as counsellors. So, it is usually not hard to find reasons for the discrepancy when we note that our practice is different from what we intended. It may be very difficult to perform our jobs as we think they should be done when organizational frames stand in the way, as they often do. Not infrequently, we have to realize that there is too little time, that the economy presents problems of finance, that the attitudes of colleagues and superiors are unfavourable etc. The intentions presented above may therefore appear unrealistic or even idealistic for the work of a counsellor in a specific organization.

Perhaps they are. Perhaps it is impossible to counsel in a productive way in many real life surroundings. If that is the case, we should all be honest and admit that productive counselling is not possible here and now. We should also be honest in not using others (the organization, the teachers etc.) as alibis, putting the blame more on them than on ourselves. It is so easy to take existing conditions as unchangeable and make our practice fit them. But we should also ask ourselves the question: Is this what we want to do, to work as professional counsellors in a way we consider to be inadequate just because outside factors make it difficult?

It has been said that the optimist thinks that this is the best of all possible worlds. The pessimist knows it is! As optimists of another sort, we think that this world may even be improved, at least as far as counselling is concerned. Our strategy for improving it may now be summarized from another point of view than that which has been presented so far.

It has been our major postulate that every person who teaches has a practical educational theory of her own. When confronted with a teaching task, she will have some hypotheses as to how the teaching might be performed. An inexperienced teacher will probably have a limited number of these hypotheses; while an experienced one will possess a variety, readily available. From her stock of hypotheses the teacher will pick out one that seems to be best, bearing in mind the nature of the task and its context (pupil characteristics, objectives, frames etc). To some, a figure may illustrate the point (see Figure 7.1):

In the figure, the upper part deals with hypothetical entities at an intentional level. It illustrates the mental activity of a teacher before a teaching session. Pre-teaching counselling deals with the relationship between the teacher's practical educational theory, the process-intentions of some of her hypotheses and the objectives of the teaching task.

What the counsellor tries to do, in this phase of the counselling process, is to help the teacher clarify these relationships, to help her become more detailed and specific in developing her process-intentions and to expand her repertoire of hypotheses. Pre-teaching counselling may be characterized as a didactic analysis of one teaching unit on the basis of the present educational theory of the teacher in question.

The lower part of the figure contains some of the major elements of the teaching unit as it turns out in practice. Post-teaching counselling deals with the relationship between the intended process and results and the actual process and results,

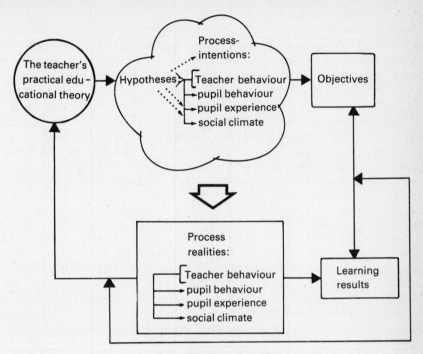

Figure 7.1
The counselling process.

comparing realities with intentions. When only minor discrepancies are identified between objectives and learning results, the performance of the teacher can be said to be appropriate. Still, even here it is very important to compare the process-intentions with the actual process itself. The valuable question here is: why did it turn out so *well*?

Usually there are discrepancies to be found. They should not be used *against* the teacher. They present the major learning potential to be found in this kind of situation.

The main objective in counselling is to provide the teacher with feedback for the improvement of her practical theory. Whatever a teaching unit may present as regards learning potential (from both successes and failures) should be made to bear on the practical theory. This is what counselling is about. This is how the teacher's theory can be elaborated, expanded and corrected; then made more relevant, useful and ready to hand for her.

The figure is not meant to imply any rigid teacher behaviour. Process-intentions should certainly be fairly detailed. However, during the session the teacher may find them inappropriate. When this is the case, it is definitely not prescribed that the teacher should stick to her plans and carry them out regardless. On the contrary, when she deems it appropriate to perform her teaching in a different manner to that planned, she should do so, thereby furnishing the counselling with especially interesting material. What made her change her plans? Why were the original process-intentions inadequate? What new process-intentions did she decide on there and then? How did they turn out?

At the end, we should like to say a few words about labels. We have tried to put our own labels on the strategy presented and the philosophy behind it. We have tried to differentiate between the labels that refer to teaching and those that refer to counselling, although the two have, as we have seen, to be related. The figure above shows the major concern we have given to the practical educational theory of teachers we work with as counsellors. The role of the counsellor is always that of helping teachers to improve *their* theory on the basis of their own experience and value positions, with the help of a conceptual scheme. We label this approach 'humanistic', from an assumption of the ability of each teacher to achieve self-improvement and independence. We can leave you with the last of many questions: Is this a naive and idealistic assumption or is it true to the reality of your own counselling experience?

References

Arfwedson, G. (1979) *Lärares arbete. (Teachers' work.)* Studies in Curriculum Theory and Cultural Reproduction / 5. Stockholm Institute of Education.

Arfwedson, G. (1985) *School Codes and Teachers' Work. Three studies on teacher work contexts.* Studies in Curriculum Theory and Cultural Reproduction / 11. Stockholm Institute of Education. Malmö, CWK Gleerup.

Bateson, G. (1980) *Mind and Nature. A Necessary Unit.* London, Fontana.

Bateson, G. (1972) *Steps to an Ecology of Mind.* London, Intertext Books.

Bernstein, B. (1971) *Class, Codes and Control.* Vol. 3. London, Routledge & Kegan Paul.

Berg, G. and Wallin, E. (1983) *Skolan i ett utvecklingsperspektiv. (The school in a developmental perspective.)* Lund, Studentlitteratur.

Bruner, J.S. (1960) *The Process of Education.* Cambridge, Mass., XVII, 97.

Bue, T. (1973) *Pedagogisk veiledning. (Educational Supervision.)* Oslo, NKS-forlaget.

Cerf, B. (1960) *Out on a Limerick.* N.Y., Pocket Books.

Dahllöf, U. (1968) Målanalys vid planlaggning av akademisk utbildning. (Analysis of Objectives in the Planning of Academic Study Programmes.) In Thomsen, O.B. (ed.) *Universitetspedagogiske studier.* Odense, Odense University Press.

Dewey, J. (1904) The relation of theory to practice in education. *The Third yearbook of the NSSE*, Part 1. Chicago.

Eisner, E.W. (1975) The Perceptive Eye: *Toward the Reformation of Educational Evaluation.* Invited address, AERA, Wash.

Entwistle, H. (1971) The Relationships between Theory and Practice. In Tibble, J.W. (ed.) *An Introduction to the Study of Education.* London, Routledge & Kegan Paul.

Goldhammer, R., Anderson, R.H. and Krajewski, R.J. (1980) *Clinical Supervision. Special Methods for the Supervision of Teachers.* 2nd edition. N.Y., Holt, Rinehart & Winston.

Handal, G., Holmström, L.-G. and Thomsen, O.B. (eds.) (1973) *Universitetsundervisning. Problem — empiri — teori. (Teaching at Universities. Problems — empirical findings — theories.)* Lund, Studentlitteratur.

Heap, K.K. (1979) *Faglig veiledning i sosiono — utdanningen. (Subject Based Counselling in the Training of Social Workers.)* Oslo, Universitetsforlaget.

Hellesnes, J. (1975) *Sosialisering og teknokrati. (Socialization and Technocracy.)* Oslo, Glydendal.

Henriksen, H. (1978) *Undervisningens samtale. (The Dialogue of Teaching.)* Copenhagen, Christian Ejlers' Forlag.

Jackson, P. (1968) *Life in Classrooms*. N.Y., Holt, Rinehart & Winston.

Kierkegaard, S. (1906) *Synspunktet for min forfatter-virksomhed. En ligefrem meddelelse. Rapport til historien.* (*The viewpoint of my Authorship. A Frank Statement. Report to the History.*) Collected works, Vol. 6. Copenhagen, Gyldendalske bogforlag.

Lewis, A.J. and Miel, A. (1972) *Supervision for Improved Instruction: New Challenges.* Belmont, Wadsworth.

Lortie, D.C. (1975) *Schoolteacher. A Sieciological Study.* Chicago, Univ. of Chicago Press.

Lundgren, U.P. (1972) *Frame Factors and the Teaching Process. A Contribution to Curriculum Theory and Theory on Teaching.* Stockholm, Almqvist & Wiksell.

Løvlie, L. (1972) Universitetspedagogikk — eller debatten som ble vekk. (Teaching at Universities — or the debate that disappeared.) In Mediaas, N. *et al.* (eds.) *Etablert pedagogikk — makt eller avmakt?* Oslo, Universitetsforlaget.

Løvlie, L. (1974) Pedagogisk filosofi for praktiserende lærere. (Philosophy of Education for Practising Teachers.) *Pedagogen*, No. 1, 22, pp. 19–36.

Mediaas, N. *et al.* (eds.) (1972) *Etablert pedagogikk — makt eller avmakt?* (*The Dominant School of Education — omnipotence or impotence?*) Oslo, Universitetsforlaget.

Michelet, S., Bjørgum Larsen, A. and Handal, G. (1981) *Pedagogiske brokker i universitetsstudiene.* (*Elements of Pedagogy in University Study Programmes.*) Mimeographed Bulletin: SPATAK, No. 7. Institute for Educational Research, University of Oslo.

Nielsen, F. (1977) *Pædagogisk Teori og Praksis. Om pædagogisk realisme, pædagogisk humanisme og kritisk pædagogik.* (*Educational Theory and Practice. On Educational Realism, Educational Humanism and Critical Pedagogy.*) Copenhagen, Borgen.

Piaget, J. (1954) *The Construction of Reality in the Child.* Toronto, Clarke, Irwin.

Rossiter, C.M. Jr. and Pearce, W.B. (1975) *Communicating Personally. A Theory of Interpersonal Communication and Human Relationships.* Indiana, Bobbs-Merrill.

Ryle, G. (1945) Knowing How and Knowing That. *Proceedings of the Aristotelian Society, XLVI*, 6, pp. 1–16.

Sarason, S.B. (1971) *The Culture of the School and the Problem of Change.* Boston, Allyn & Bacon.

Sjöberg, C. (1977) *Klassens liv.* (Life of the Class.) Stockholm, Raben & Sjogren.

Stake, R. (1967) The Countenance of Educational Evaluation. *Teachers College Record*, 68, pp. 523–540.

Stenhouse, L. (1975) *An Introduction to Curriculum Research and Development.* London, Heinemann.

Stenhouse, L. (1979) *Research as a Basis for Teaching.* Inaugural Lecture. University of East Anglia, Norwich.

Stone, E. (1984) *Supervision in Teacher Education. A Counselling and Pedagogical Approach.* London, Methuen.

Thomsen, O.B. (ed.) (1968) *Universitetspædagogiske studier.* (*Studies on Staff Development in Universities.*) Odense, Odense University Press.

Thomsen, O.B. (1973) Universitetet i samfundet. (*The University in the Society.*) In Handal, G., Holmström, L.-G. and Thomsen, O.B. (eds.) Universitetsundervisning. Problem — empiri — teori. Lund, Studentlitteratur.

Thomsen, O.B. (1975) *Vurdering og vejledning af lærere i undervisningspraktik.* (*Appraising and Supervising Teachers in Teaching Practice.*) Institute for Applied Staff Development at Universities, University of Copenhagen. Mimeographed Report.

Tibble, J.W. (ed.) (1971) *An Introduction to the Study of Education.* London, Routledge & Kegan Paul.

Watzlawick, P., Beavin, J.H. and Jackson, D.D. (1967) *Pragmatics of Human Communication.* N.Y., Norton.

Watzlawick, P., Weakland, J.H. and Fish, R. (1974) *Change: Principles of Problem Formation and Problem Resolution.* N.Y., Norton.

Watzlawick, P. (1976) *How Real is Real? Confusion, Disinformation, Communication.* N.Y., Vintage Books.

Index

accommodation 58, 59
action 11, 26
aims and objectives 17, 33–34,
    44–45, 47, 76–77
assessment 96
assimilation 58, 59

chameleon effect/game vii, 50
certification 41, 65, 96
code 14, 16
communication 67–72
   analogue 70
   content aspect 67
   digital 70
   double communication 56, 70, 72,
    90
   meaning 68
   meta-communication 56, 67–72,
    94
   relationship aspects 67
confrontation 31, 56–61
connoiseurship 62
consultancy service 95, 99
counselling
   applications 36, 95
   climate 45, 94
   content 73
   criteria 3–4, 41
   document 30–35, 93
   in groups 39, 98–99
   initial phase 37
   mutual 102
   objective 44, 107
   phases 31, 36–43

postteaching 39–40, 83, 93,
   106–107
preteaching 38–39, 83, 93, 106
roles 9, 25, 62–64, 108
'safety net' 61
strategy 2, 5, 6, 30, 32, 36, 73, 87,
   90, 93, 105
conviction 25
courses, application in 99–102
critical approach 6
critique 61–62

dialectics 4, 6
dialogue, discourse 55–56
didactical analysis 38, 76, 80
discussion, debate 55
dissemination 96

'emergency break' 88
ethical justifications 26
evaluation, criteria 96–97
examplary principle 37, 52–55, 93

frames 15, 23, 29, 79–80

humanism 6, 108
humiliating positivism 56, 89

independence 51
instrumentalism 75

justifications 28

organizational factors 95

personal problems 97
perspectives 73, 81
   culture 83–84
   ideology 54, 85–86
   intention/effects 81–82
   micro/macro 85
   roles 35, 84
   socialization 54, 83–84
persuasion 25
practical theory 9–19, 28–30, 44, 51,
      90, 106
   components in 10–13
   consciousness of 16–17
   lack of 91–92
   of teaching 24, 106
   of counselling 46–47
practice 25–29
process intentions 33–36, 91–93, 101,
      107
   for counselling 45–47
purposes and functions 33, 34, 43,
      44, 46

reasons 27–28
reflection 11, 26, 97
reinforcement, positive 89

relationships 73–76
   subject–object 75
   symmetry/asymetry 25, 76

situational factors 21–22
strategy 13, 22, 34
superficiality 76
support 39, 57, 60

teacher intentions 32
teacher training 95
   preschool 93
teaching practice 95
teaching unit 93, 100
   artificial 95, 99
teaching realities 32
themes 73, 76
   content 77
   evaluation 79
   frame factors 79
   interrelations 80
   pupil characteristics 78
   purpose, aims 76
   teaching methods 77
theory and practice 4, 31–32

value differences 45–46, 69

The Society for Research into Higher Education

The Society exists both to encourage and co-ordinate research and development into all aspects of Higher Education, including academic, organizational and policy issues; and also to provide a forum for debate, verbal and printed. Through its activities, it draws attention to the significance of research into, and development in, Higher Education and to the needs of scholars in this field. (It is not concerned with research generally, except, for instance, as a subject of study.)

The Society's income derives from subscriptions, book sales, conferences and specific grants. It is wholly independent. Its corporate members are institutions of higher education, research institutions and professional, industrial, and governmental bodies. Its individual members include teachers and researchers, administrators and students. Members are found in all parts of the world and the Society regards its international work as amongst its most important activities.

The Society discusses and comments on policy, organizes conferences and encourages research. Under the Imprint SRHE & OPEN UNIVERSITY PRESS, it is a specialist publisher, having some 40 titles in print. It also publishes *Studies in Higher Education* (three times a year) which is mainly concerned with academic issues, *Higher Education Quarterly* (formerly *Universities Quarterly*) which will be mainly concerned with policy issues, *Research into Higher Education Abstracts* (three times a year), and a *Bulletin* (six times a year).

The Society's committees, study groups and branches are run by members (with help from a small staff at Guildford), and aim to provide a form for discussion. The groups at present include a Teacher Education Study Group, a Staff Development Group, a Women in Higher Education Group and a Continuing Education Group which may have had their own organization, subscriptions or publications; (eg the *Staff Development Newsletter*). The Governing Council, elected by members, comments on current issues; and discusses policies with leading figures, notably at its evening Forums. The Society organizes seminars on current research for officials of DES and other ministries, an Anglo-American series on standards, and is in touch with bodies in the UK such as the NAB, CVCP, UGC, CNAA and the British Council, and with sister-bodies overseas. Its current research projects include one on the relationship between entry qualifications and degree results, directed by Prof. W. D. Furneaux (Brunel) and one on questions of quality directed by Prof. G. C. Moodie (York). A project on the evaluation of the research standing of university departments is in preparation. The Society's conferences are often held jointly. Annual Conferences have considered 'Professional Education' (1984), 'Continuing Education' (1985, with Goldsmiths' College) 'Standards and Citeria in Higher Education'

(1986, with Bulmershe CHE), 'Restructuring' (1987, with the City of Birmingham Polytechnic) and 'Academic Freedom' (1988, the University of Surrey). Other conferences have considered the DES 'Green Paper' (1985, with the Times Higher Education Supplement), and 'The First-Year Experience' (1986, with the University of South Carolina and Newcastle Polytechnic). For some of the Society's conferences, special studies are commissioned in advance, as 'Precedings'.

Members receive free of charge the Society's *Abstracts*, annual conference Proceedings (or 'Precedings'), *Bulletin and International Newsletter* and may buy SRHE & OPEN UNIVERSITY PRESS books at booksellers' discount. Corporate members also receive the Society's journal *Studies in Higher Education* free (individuals at a heavy discount). They may also obtain *Evaluation Newsletter* and certain other journals at a discount, including the NFER *Register of Educational Research*. There is a substantial discount to members, and to staff of corporate members, on annual and some other conference fees.